Caught in the Grip of Political Correctness

Caught in the Grip of

POLITICAL CORRECTNESS

Fred DeRuvo

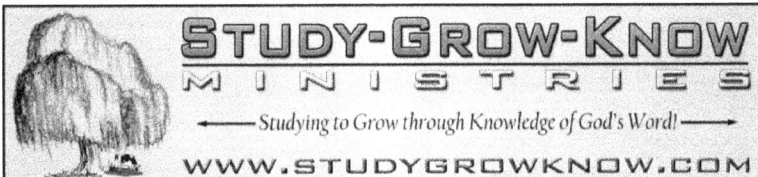

Published in Scotts Valley, California, by Adroit Publications
www.studygrowknow.com • www.studygrowknowblog.com

Unless otherwise noted, Scripture quotations taken from the New American Standard Bible®, Copyright © 1960, 1962, 1963, 1968, 1971, 1972, 1973, 1975, 1977, 1995 by The Lockman Foundation. Used by permission. (www.Lockman.org)

All Woodcuts used herein are in the Public Domain and free of copyright.

All Figure illustrations used in this book were created by the author and protected under copyright laws, © 2013.

Edited by: Hannah Brady

Library of Congress Cataloging-in-Publication Data

DeRuvo, Fred, 1957 –

ISBN 098818334X
EAN-978-0-9881833-4-6

1. Political Science / Political Ideologies / Communism & Socialism

"For my mouth will utter truth;
And wickedness is an abomination to my lips" – Proverbs 8:7

Contents

Foreword

In my most recent book – *Falling Away* – I dealt with a topic that, in truth, cannot be covered in one book. In essence, that previous book probably laid a foundation for this one.

The importance of *political correctness* cannot be overstated. It seems that it is too often *understated* though. So many areas in society have been affected by some aspect of political correctness that it is difficult to think of an area that has not been impacted by it.

In an effort to continue the education we began in *The Great Falling Away*, I have chosen to include in this book areas of political correctness that I either did not cover at all previously or did not cover thoroughly enough. Once a person realizes the true scope of political correctness and how deeply enmeshed within society it has become, it can do one of two things (or both):

1. Cause a person to feel free to simply be themselves because understanding the nature of political correctness means no longer being subjugated by it, or
2. Cause a person to realize that aside from overcoming it on a personal level, there is not a great deal that can be done about it.

As I say, a person may feel a deep sense of the first one or the second and at times may alternate between them both. While understanding what has worked its way into society is freeing, it can also be a bit overwhelming. It leaves one feeling as though little if anything can be done to overcome what has taken over society.

However, I believe that people cannot give up the ship. We can and should continue to resist the effects of political correctness. There will be things we cannot successfully resist that have to do with the way government runs and the steps it seeks to remove our freedoms, many of which we have taken for granted.

At the same time, if we can resist it to the point that other people's eyes are open to the realities of political correctness and how much sway it has gained over our nation – America – then that is a good thing.

You see, I'm an individual who strongly believes that being swept along by political correctness has made it very difficult to see God's truth. His truth, of course, is absolute, unlike political correctness, which is nothing more than a form of humanistic relativism. If you read my last book, then you already know that.

I'm hopeful that win or lose, people will cast off the political correctness and all of its tragic results. It is to this end that this book is written.

- Fred DeRuvo, October 2013

Chapter 1

Gramsci, Marx, Engel and the New Left

I was almost done with this book when I came across a book that discussed meanings and history related to Karl Marx and his partner Friedrich Engels. Author Zuriel Redwood (*Minority Bolshevism*) also discloses information related to Communism, Socialism, and even what he calls "Minority Bolshevism," all of this leading to today's political correctness.

Rather than simply be done with my book, I thought it best to add a chapter using information based on Redwood's book as a means to lay the groundwork for what I cover in this book. It's an interesting book and one that every conservative should have in his library.

Minority Bolshevism is killing America. I've read a number of books on Communism, Socialism, and Marxism and you probably have as well. However, author Zuriel Redwood seems to be able to put things together remarkably well (and concisely) in a book that helps us understand just exactly how these ideologies have gotten us to the point where we are at now and what's in store for us if we continue down this path.

Redwood notes, *"This book is about the wrong tracks and the people who designed them, who built them and who are peddling the one-way tickets. Minority Bolshevism is the ideology responsible for diverting our future onto the wrong tracks. Minority Bolshevism is killing America."*[1]

Redwood doesn't spend a good deal of time breaking everything down into minutiae so that the reader gets bored before he reaches the conclusion. Instead, Redwood is more concerned about concise, useful explanations that allow people to understand that piece of the puzzle, then that other piece of the puzzle, and then the next. Soon, the entire puzzle is starting to take shape. Rather than focusing solely on one or two pieces of the puzzle, Redwood uses the various pieces to help build the completed picture.

While Redwood provides an overview – or history and development – of Marxism, Communism, and Socialism, leading to what he calls the New Left, he does so only to show how things got to be the way they are now, especially in America. You've likely read about the Countercultural Movement of the 1960s, the Anti-War protests, and many things that have become part of this nation's undeniable history and fabric. It has all worked toward a minority Bolshevism and he explains that in his book.

---

[1] http://minoritybolshevism.com/?page_id=28 (05/27/2013)

Marx *"advocated the violent overthrow of capitalism and all class-based societies."*[2] He also advocated political power against economic power. One can easily see that those who hold political power also oversee economic power in many ways. Moreover, together with friend and comrade Friedrich Engels, he *"decided that religion and the family also had to be destroyed."*[3] These were considered to be "ancient and oppressive traditions." They needed to go. But how to accomplish it?

Marx truly saw the need for a violent revolution and was sorely disappointed when the Parisian Proletariat did not follow through and actually kill the ruling class but preferred organizing elections instead. After a short time, this same proletariat was put down by France's armies, thus ending the first successful revolution.

Intellectual Antonio Gramsci was a life-long Italian communist, whose writings (while in prison) came to be the foundation for the New Left of today. It was learned that upon his death in prison (in 1937), he left the world with 1,800 pages of writings that reflected his intellectualism with respect to Communism and the fight against Capitalism.

Instead of looking to the "proletariat" to carry the torch for revolution (they had learned to compromise with the business titans of his day – something he called "Fordism"), he set out to find new groups of people whose discontent could be fanned into flame. This flame – he hoped – would well up into a full-fledged conflagration that would catapult them to victory against the bourgeois – capitalists!

Who were these new groups of people? Gramsci *"identified homosexuals, radical feminists, racial minorities and criminals, among others, as potential allies in this fight. He also thought it would be more feasi-*

[2] Redwood, Zuriel (2012-08-29). Minority Bolshevism (Kindle Lo-cations 534-535). Kindle Edition.
[3] Ibid

ble to wage this war on the field of culture. A 'culture war' seemed more winnable than economic struggle or political revolution."[4] Remember, this was in the 1930s.

Furthermore, Gramsci "*even devised a new strategy against class-based society — instead of direct confrontation and revolution, he advocated a 'long march through the institutions'. He essentially invented the idea of 'cultural revolution'.*"[5]

What is fascinating is that, though Gramsci died in prison never seeing his dreams come true, they began to come to fruition through an American president by the name of Franklin Delano Roosevelt (FDR), a Democrat and progressive whose programs created much of the foundation for coming ideals. Interestingly enough, "*soon after becoming President he recognized the Soviet Union (USSR) and made a deal to settle all cases of Soviet expropriation of American property. He did not bother to send the agreement to the Senate for ratification.*"[6] The fact that FDR totally bypassed Congress reminds me of another president who seems to enjoy doing the same thing. Ah, who needs Congress?

The 1960s officially introduced the "cultural revolution" to America. America was in Vietnam. New "rock and roll" music had just barely come out of its shell, only to be pushed aside by "acid music" from musicians like Jimi Hendrix, The Doors, Janis Joplin, and others. "Hippies" became a household word. As Redwood notes, "*In a single generation culture itself has changed. A decade after that it was unrecognizable.*"[7]

---

[4] Redwood, Zuriel (2012-08-29). Minority Bolshevism (Kindle Locations 653-656). Kindle Edition.
[5] Ibid
[6] Ibid, Locations 672-673
[7] Ibid, Location 809

People who did not live through this tumultuous change will never understand it. They will only be able to see it from afar, not ever truly understanding the impact those changes had on America and the world. Activism became socially acceptable, and because of that, change was expected.

This has all led to the pinnacle of the New Left Ideal: political correctness, which is not based on any absolute truth, but based on emotional virtue. If it feels good, it must be right. If it feels good, do it. As Redwood opines, *"Political correctness is a devastating weapon that attacks our very ability to think clearly about the most important issues of the day. It prevents us from making the right decisions. It defeats us before the battle even began."*[8]

The New Left has as its purpose the old ideas of Karl Marx and Friedrich Engels. They have simply found the way to recreate those ideas so that they accomplish what Marx intended while going about it in a completely unique way.

I can list any number of books that will teach you about Marxism, Communism, or Socialism. But this book is written to clearly achieve its intended goal of deciphering what these things are and how they have been at work to change global society.

As you continue reading through this book, hopefully it will give you a greater understanding of how I connect the dots. For more information, I would strongly suggest purchasing Redwood's book, either in Kindle or paperback format. It's well worth it, if for no other reason than as a primer on Karl Marx and what he tried and hoped to accomplish. We can thank him for the fact that the New Left exists today, if that's something for which we can actually be thankful.

---

[8] Redwood, Zuriel (2012-08-29). Minority Bolshevism (Kindle Locations 1052-1054). Kindle Edition.

Chapter 2

Politically Correct Love

The following comments are attributed to a retired USMC Vet. Whether this is the case or not, I cannot be sure. However, these words – as far as I can see – are the epitome of truth and need to be shared repeatedly by people who also love truth. They highlight what political correctness has caused to occur in society.

The American Dream ended (on November 6th) in Ohio.
The second term of Barack Obama will be the final nail in
the coffin for the legacy of the white Christian males who
discovered, explored, pioneered, settled and developed the
greatest Republic in the history of mankind.

A coalition of Blacks, Latinos, Feminists, Gays, Government Workers, Union Members, Environmental Extremists, The Media, Hollywood, uninformed young people, the "forever needy," the chronically unemployed, illegal aliens and other "fellow travelers" have ended Norman Rockwell's America.

The Cocker Spaniel is off the front porch...the Pit Bull is in the back yard.

The American Constitution has been replaced with Saul Alinsky's Rules for Radicals and Chicago shyster, David Axelrod, along with international Socialist George Soros will be pulling the strings on their beige puppet to bring us Act 2 of the New World Order.

Our side ran two candidates who couldn't even win their own home states, and the circus fatty Chris Christie helped Obama over the top with a glowing "post Sandy" tribute that elevated the "Commander-in-Chief" to Mother Teresa status.

People like me are completely politically irrelevant, and I will never again comment on or concern myself with the afore-mentioned coalition which has surrendered our culture, our heritage and our traditions without a shot being fired.

You will never again out vote these people. It will take individual acts of defiance and massive displays of civil disobedience to get back the rights we have allowed them to take away. It will take Zealots, not moderates--not reach-across-the-aisle RINOs to right this ship and restore our beloved country to its former status.

> *Those who come after us will have to risk their lives, their fortunes and their sacred honor to bring back the Republic that this generation has timidly frittered away due to "white guilt" and political correctness...*

> *I'm done.*

Too many people are blind to these truths; many of them are young and have not grown up during the time this Vet refers to, nor have they ever had to fight for these truths. Because actual American history is not taught (except the politically correct version of it), folks do not truly understand how things were and how far we have come from them.

I can appreciate this man's frustration and he paints a terribly dark future picture, but it is not that different from what we learn in Scripture about the days ahead. I understand why he says he is "done."

We must keep warning people whether anyone likes it or not (especially the PC crowd). We need to do this, if for no other reason than to show that the 1st Amendment still applies to all people, not simply those they deem "victims."

To those who claim to be Christian and are comfortably established deep within the mire of political correctness, I cannot help but hope that if they will only take a few moments to thoroughly engage with God in prayer, asking Him to show them the fallacious nature of the things they believe, their eyes might open.

If we can say anything about political correctness, we can say that it is – at least sometimes – guided along by a genuine desire to help, but its help is little more than a form of disingenuous "feel-good love" that actually lacks the true love that God demands. It is a love based on emotional pull and not based on God's truth.

We spent much time in my last book going over aspects of political correctness, critical race theory, and Cultural Marxism, determining the "victim" and the "aggressor" in numerous situations. I tried to show that political correctness actually attempts to destroy God's truth by setting it aside, replacing it with the relativism of emotional virtue.

Of course, those within the politically correct arena would disagree. But, due to the double standard that is created in society through the relativistic process of deciding "victim" from "aggressor," it becomes clear that the same "truth" that is used to declare one person a "victim" is not the same truth that is used to declare someone else an "aggressor."

Certain individuals automatically fall into the "victim" category, based solely on their ethnicity or minority status. Thus, a black person (or other person of color) is essentially categorized as a "victim" all the time.

This is also why when a person of color "comes out" as a conservative, they are panned, labeled, castigated, and more. They are called "house Negroes" if they are black, implying that they are blind to the fact that they are being used by the GOP or some other conservative (mainly white) group. It is unthinkable that a person of color could actually have conservative values and so they are obviously blind.

However, I and many others would argue that those persons of color within the politically correct arena are the ones who are being used by the liberal elite. They are the true "house Negroes" if any exist. They are being kept on the plantation, in Section 8 housing, and they receive their "pay" in the form of government-sponsored welfare checks. Is this a form of "reparations" for the slavery that blacks endured (and they would argue, still endure)? After all, these blacks are the "victims." Nothing they can be given is too much.

Of course, in order to be a victim, they must be compared with something else, usually what is believed to be the "white power structure." In that case, it becomes easy to discern the "victim" from the "aggressor." When women are added to the mix, it is even more clearly defined by placing them up against the white male only. In almost all cases, the white male is seen to be the "aggressor" who routinely leaves a swath of "victims" in his wake.

So, white males who endeavor to not be seen as the "aggressor" must go out of their way to visibly side with "victims." In that way then, they "save" themselves from being treated harshly by the rest of the politically correct in society. They are fully absolved of responsibility because they are seen as trying to make "amends" by siding with the "victim" against other white males (conservatives, right-wingers, and extremists) who are allegedly determined to hold them down.

Note that in these types of situations, those white men do all they can to perform for the "victim" so that they will be thought of as enlightened and therefore not repugnant to the "victim." However, these white males must be constantly in "self-emasculation" mode. They must actively put themselves (and all other white males) down, blamed as the essential problem-creators of society. As long as they continue to do that, they will be accepted by the "victims." It is a form of penitence referred to as "self-loathing," made possible and encouraged by "white guilt." For the white male, this thinking and expected attitude is deeply engrained within the politically correct mentality. The politically correct can do no better than to have white males as spokespersons: their trophy. This actively portrays the white male as the "aggressor" who has seen the error of his ways and is deeply contrite because of it, desperately wanting to make amends.

Biblically, these white men who claim to be Christian and are deeply embedded in the Cultural Marxism of our day (through political correctness) have a unique view of Scripture, especially the interaction of Jesus with the religious leaders. For many white males of this order (especially *young* white males), the narrative in the gospels presents a picture of the bourgeois against the proletariat. It is the "aggressor" lording it over the "victim."

In this case, obviously, Jesus represents the "victim" against the elitist religious leader, the "aggressor." This class struggle breeds contempt through fear: fear on the side of the average person who is afraid to stand up to the religious leader. Jesus – a political figure (and politically correct) – resists them and their fear-induced slavery.

At every turn, Jesus – using political correctness to right wrongs (so it is alleged) – opposes the religious leaders. Jesus is not afraid to speak with a Samaritan woman (cf. John 4), against tradition. There is nothing in the Mosaic Law that said He could not speak with a Samaritan woman in a public place. That belief had developed from hatred of Samaritans during the time between the testaments when the sect of the Pharisees first came into being.

Jesus withstands a group of individuals who want to stone a woman to death, who they say was caught in the act of adultery (cf. John 8). The men represent the "right-wing extremists" of the day and Jesus rebuked them.

In essence, what Jesus rebuked was the legalism of society and the abject lack of care and concern. He did not set aside Biblical Law as some would have us believe. Adultery was punishable by death during the time of Moses and during the time of Jesus. All Jesus did was ensure that every part of the Mosaic Law was upheld correctly.

In Deuteronomy 13:9 and 17:7, we learn that those who accused someone of a crime (in this case, adultery) were also to have been witnesses of it (as the text implies they were). Moreover, the Mosaic Law ensured that only those people who had not been found guilty of the same sin themselves could participate in carrying out the sentence for that crime.

At the very least, Jesus' words caused these men, who were ready to kill the woman, to think seriously about the ramifications of what they were about to do and about their own lives. Notice that Jesus at no time told them to NOT carry out the lawful sentence prescribed by the Mosaic Law.

The politically correct take the situation in John 8 as an example that Christians are to go through life never pointing out sin because that's called "being judgmental" and we should not judge (cf. Matthew 7 – deals with judging motives, not actions or words). We are to "love" people, which to these folks means never saying a discouraging word, never even evidencing a hint of displeasure at the actions or words of another (unless they are considered to be the "aggressor" toward a "victim"). Christians – to these folks – are to be the epitome of smiles, laughter, acceptance, and love. All of this is, unfortunately, based on *emotion*, not *truth*.

The problem, as we've discussed before, is that political correctness does not engender true justice. PC goals are "equality" and "freedom," but only for those determined to be "victims." God, on the other hand, seeks justice, and that is what He calls us to seek. Justice gives people what they deserve, not necessarily what they feel they deserve or even want.

God loves because He *is* love. He is also just, holy, and a plethora of other adjectives. He can no more love people separate from absolute justice than I can separate from air and live. Yet the politically correct religious person believes the emphasis should be on "love," and of course, their love is defined by emotionally determining "victim" from "aggressor." That has nothing to do with God's love.

Political correctness is tearing society down by pitting "victims" against "aggressors." It troubles me greatly to see people who call themselves Christian participating in PC attitudes.

This is not what Christians are called to do. We are called to be a light in society for the gospel, not add to its darkness. In the coming days, the gulf between light and dark will become even more noticeable. I pray you and I are prepared for it, in the strength of His Presence in our lives.

Chapter 3

Politically Correct Gun Control

The argument from the politically correct left regarding gun control is, like all issues they deal with, fundamentally over-simplified. They start with a premise and go from there. It does not even matter whether or not their premise is based on truth. It only has to *appear* to be truthful and that's good enough.

For the politically correct and the issue of guns, their premise is that guns are bad because guns kill people. Simple. It paints *guns* as evil, so what could be better? Well, the actual truth, for one.

When the politically correct charge guns are bad because they kill people, they are obviously *not* referring to guns used by law en-forcement officers. They also cannot be referring to guns used by law-abiding citizens against criminals either, though they tend to gloss over things here.

The politically correct crowd essentially tries to paint a picture showing that if guns did not exist in society, they could not kill people. Certainly, if *no* guns had ever been created, this would be true, but it also does not mean that people killing other people would end.

So, in keeping with their defective premise, they work to eradicate guns from society by lying, all the while telling people that they *respect* the 2nd Amendment. They assure us that what they are attempting to do will not ban guns from society but simply make things safer for all people. They promise that they only want to take guns away from criminals, not law-abiding citizens. Unfortunately, all the laws they want to enact only affect law-abiding citizens. Then again, their premise – like much of the way they deal with serious issues in society – is faulty at best.

First of all, guns do not kill people. If we want to be technical, bullets kill people. But even apart from that, it is the *people* who wield guns that actually kill people when they pull the trigger.

No one says that cars kill people, even when driven by drunks. We always hear about drunk *drivers* who kill people, and rarely is the car ever mentioned. Drunks are the ones who are arrested for drunk driving. While the car can be impounded, the car itself does not spend the night in a jail cell or get charged with a felony in a court of law. It's the person who owns the car or operated the car while intoxicated that is arrested. Even if the car hits another person and kills them, the driver is the one who is arrested because of it. The newspapers do not report that another car killed someone last night as if the car had a mind all its own.

However, this is exactly what the politically correct attempt to do where guns are concerned. They *want* people to think that guns have a mind of their own and like some B-rated horror movie can sneak out of the drawer or closet and take you out when you least expect it.

Another problem within politically correct circles regarding guns is the oft-heard mantra that if passing new laws saves even one life, well then it's worth it (sniff). This simply proves that the politically correct make their decisions based not on *absolute truth*, but on *emotional virtue*, as if bringing people to tears because of a supposed earnest desire to save one life assumes an altruistic reason.

But let's face it, kids have been killing each other on the streets of our big cities for decades: whites, blacks, Hispanics, and Asians. Guns are the weapon of choice for gang members going back to the 1950s and before. Politicians do not talk about these kids. They aren't interested in saving them. But I thought saving even one was worth it?

Those within politically correct circles refuse to discuss the fact that, while guns are used by people to commit crimes, guns are also used by law-abiding citizens to save lives. This is the *real* inconvenient truth that the gun-grabbers within the politically correct subculture do not want to admit exists. Guns are used to keep people safe.

People with guns have saved life by using a gun to thwart a home invasion, a car-jacking, or a robbery. Not long ago, in North Georgia, a man wound up breaking into a home in broad daylight. The woman inside the home saw and heard the man knocking on her door and refused to open it for him. Instead, she took her two young children (twin nine-year-olds) and herself and hid in a closet upstairs with a loaded revolver.

Not long afterwards, the man broke the front door in. The woman called her husband (who called 9-1-1) and as the intruder opened the door where the woman was hiding with her children, she opened fire on him. He sustained five gunshots to the chest, neck, and face and apparently survived.

What if she had not had a revolver with her? It was clear that the woman wanted to avoid a confrontation with the intruder, which is why she hid in the first place. Legally, in Georgia, she could have simply waited until he smashed through the front door and shot him, but she chose to hide instead, hoping that if he came in, he would leave quickly or the police would be there soon.

So, the question is, whose life did that woman save that day? She obviously saved her own and the lives of her two children. Isn't that what politicians for gun control always complain about: saving just "one" life? Well, that woman saved *three* that day. I would prefer not to think about what the intruder might have done to the woman had she had no way of defending herself.

So the statement that they want to save a life is really disingenuous because neither the politically correct media nor the politically correct politicians ever talk about how guns are used to thwart the bad guy. They only talk about the times guns are used to kill innocent people and they love to parade these people before the media and Congress. This tells you their agenda.

There are many incidents every year in which law-abiding citizens legally use a firearm to protect life and liberty. If we listen to PC politicians and non-politicians alike, obviously the life of that mother in Georgia (or her twins) was not worth saving. How dare she have a gun!

Even the media plays their politically correct games in the hopes of persuading people that most of America believes semi-auto weapons should be banned. If you listen to their lies, 74% of NRA members apparently "*support a ban on semi-automatic firearms.*"[9]

When the NRA's Institute for Legislative Action conducted its own survey of NRA members, they came to the following conclusions:

---

[9] Freedom 1st magazine, April 2013, p. 19

- *89 percent oppose banning semi-automatic firearms, often mistakenly called "assault rifles"*
- *91 percent of NRA members support laws keeping firearms away from the mentally ill*
- *92 percent of NRA members oppose gun confiscation via mandatory buy-back laws*
- *93 percent oppose a law requiring gun owners to register with the federal government*
- *92 percent oppose a new federal law banning the sale of firearms between private citizens*[10]

Shortly after the Sandy Hook tragedy, Washington went into overtime to see what it could do to make people feel safer about guns. There was a good deal of talk among politicians about new laws that would ban guns and "high-capacity" magazines, new ideas, and even gun confiscation.

Law-abiding citizens of America started to think that maybe Washington had become filled with liberal politicians who had one thing on their minds: *taking guns from law-abiding people* or *making it next to impossible for law-abiding people to own guns or ammo.* This fear quickly translated into action through gun and ammo sales all over America. Obama became the best gun salesman ever.

Guns that were routinely referred to incorrectly as "assault rifles" flew off the store shelves and could not be kept in stock. Semi-automatic handguns and ammo became (and remain) hard to find as well.

Interestingly enough, this was blamed on the NRA for using "fear" tactics to tell people that the government was going to take their weapons. However, we know that some politicians had already gone on record by that time stating that they wanted to confiscate guns

---

[10] Freedom 1ˢᵗ magazine, April 2013, p. 19

(Gov. Cuomo, NY) or ban guns that people already owned (Sen. Dianne Feinstein, CA). The fear was introduced by *politicians*, not the *NRA.* The NRA simply wants to protect the 2nd Amendment.

This is the dishonest way politicians attempt to turn things around. In truth though, they do not see their ways as dishonest or duplicitous because they are politically correct and that means they can do no wrong, even when they lie. It's all for the cause. When you are part of the politically correct crowd, you can literally say things one way at one time, but then say them the exact opposite later on. It's all part of how the "war" is played by the politically correct.

For instance, just prior to winning his first election in 2008, Barack Obama had gone on record as saying, *"I will not take your shotgun away. I will not take your rifle away. I won't take your handgun away...I am not going to take your guns away."*[11]

Then in 2013, Obama stated, *"We should restore the ban on military-style assault weapons and a 10-round limit for magazines...because weapons of war have no place on our streets."*[12]

But let's think seriously for a moment. Do politicians actually believe that banning assault weapons or capping magazines off at ten rounds (or seven) will have any effect on the bad guys and their ability to obtain the weapons they want to have in their arsenal? No one can be that naïve, yet it appears that gun-control politicians want us to believe that banning "assault" rifles and limiting magazines *would* have an effect on the bad guy. This is absurd.

Laws against drunk driving don't keep drunks from driving. All the laws in the world have not made a dent in illicit drug use. There are even laws that keep law-abiding citizens from buying one too many boxes of Claritin-D because it contains an ingredient that could be

---

[11] Freedom 1st magazine, April 2013, p. 34
[12] Ibid

used in making illegal drugs. Once again, the law-abiding citizen suffers because of the criminal.

Recently, Piers Morgan claimed that Adam Lanza, the alleged shooter in the Sandy Hook tragedy, was a member of the NRA.[13] He tweeted the following: *"I want to hear Wayne LaPierre explain what checks they made on Adam Lanza before sending him a @nra certificate."*[14]

The stupidity of this tweet from Morgan is clear to individuals who are familiar with the powers of critical thinking. Unfortunately, the implication is that the NRA was directly involved in the gun course and the NRA was to have (according to Morgan) supposedly checked Lanza's background before they gave him a certificate.

This lie was meant to vilify the NRA. It turns out that what the police actually recovered was a booklet that had been written by the NRA as well as two certificates. The certificates issued were for having successfully completed a gun safety course given by an NRA-certified instructor.

The NRA was not involved in that training at all. The instructor was *certified* by the NRA, though not otherwise connected, but the NRA did not issue the certificates. Moreover, the certificates are given to students who successfully complete a specific gun course that day. They are not sent to them later on by the NRA.

The NRA put out their own statement saying, *"There is no record of a member relationship between Newtown killer Adam Lanza, nor be-*

---

[13] http://pjmedia.com/instapundit/165979/?utm_source=twitterfeed&utm_medium=twitter&utm_campaign=Feed%3A+pjmedia%2Finstapundit+%28Instapundit%29 (03/28/2013)

[14] http://newsbusters.org/blogs/matt-vespa/2013/03/28/cnns-piers-morgan-falsely-claims-newtown-shooter-was-nra-member#ixzz2OtnxPIkG (03/28/2013)

tween Nancy Lanza, A. Lanza or N. Lanza with the National Rifle Association. Reporting to the contrary is reckless, false and defamatory."[15]

As for doing a "background" check on Adam Lanza prior to "sending him a certificate," even if a background check *had* been done, what would have been uncovered? Nothing. He had no criminal record.

By the way, so we are clear, *anyone* can take a gun course. It is not up to the instructor to do a background check on an individual signing up for the gun class. Background checks are done *prior* to the purchase of a gun and in order to take *most* gun courses, a gun is required. The background check would have already been accomplished in order for the person to have a gun in the first place.

But this type of "reporting" from those within the politically correct media is cause for concern because it clearly shows their intent. It is not to report the news, but to *create* or *slant* the news that favors their side of the issues. Unbiased journalism is a thing of the past and political correctness has seen to that.

In a recent video ad[16] from *Mayors Against Gun Violence*, the main actor in the ad breaks several rules of good gun ownership. The actor is seen sitting in the bed of his truck with his family in the background, children playing. He is dressed in what the producers likely believed to be normal hunting gear. He looks just a bit like what some might expect a "redneck" to look like.

The actor speaks of wanting his family protected, etc., and believes that extensive background checks and a few other things will help make society a safer place. The problem with the ad is that it is diffi-

---

[15] http://newsbusters.org/blogs/matt-vespa/2013/03/28/cnns-piers-morgan-falsely-claims-newtown-shooter-was-nra-member#ixzz2OtnxPlkG (03/28/2013)

[16] http://www.mrconservative.com/2013/03/8918-michael-bloombergs-anti-gun-ad-flops-as-actor-breaks-first-two-rules-of-gun-safety/ (03/28/2013)

cult to pay attention to what he's saying because of the glaring error in the way he is holding his long gun (rifle).

The actor has the gun resting across his lap, with the barrel pointing in the same direction where his kids also happen to be playing, though behind him. Though they're in the background, it would not take much for one of the kids to run up to where "dad" is and across the front of the gun. If the gun went off, there could be serious injury or even death as a result. The gun should be pointing *down* at the ground directly in front of him, not across his lap. The other option would be to have the gun pointing directly up. The actor in the ad holds the gun in a very unsafe position.

The actor's right hand is also near the trigger area and the way he is holding his hand makes it difficult to tell whether or not he has his finger *on* the trigger, or if his entire hand is simply covering the trigger area, including the trigger guard. The plain fact of the matter is that his hand should not be anywhere *near* the trigger unless he is ready to shoot the gun. His right hand should be way back, on the butt of the gun, well away from the trigger altogether. The way he is holding the gun is how accidents happen.

What can you do, though, when you have people like Mayor Michael Bloomberg, who is so opposed to guns that he will do anything he can to get his point across? Then again, this is the same mayor who wanted to ban large drinks but was stopped by the courts. Undeterred, Bloomberg decided to go after cigarettes, insisting that they should no longer be in public view in stores that sell them. Yep, that will keep kids from ever wanting to start smoking and adults from buying them. They'll never figure out that the cigarettes are there, just out of view. Out of sight equals out of mind.

Again though, most of what the politically correct attempt to do is based on their ability to *emotionally* sway us into believing what they want us to believe. In the case of guns, they want us to believe that "saving just one life" is more important than retaining the right to keep and bear arms. It's obviously also more important than the reality that exists where guns are used to *save* lives, lives which are completely discounted (by dutifully being ignored) by the same politicians who attempt to emotionally shame us into giving up our rights.

As recently as this past March, 2013, Mr. Obama continued to give emotionally-charged speeches that were intended to cause us to hang our heads in shame over the issue of "needed" gun control and the fact that public opinion in favor of gun control was waning. One article noted, "*President Obama made an emotional plea for Congress to pass gun-control legislation, telling the political world 'shame on us' if it has forgotten the 26 people killed at Sandy Hook Elementary School less than 100 days ago.*"[17]

No one has forgotten anything about Sandy Hook or the other tragedies that have shaken America, including the worst massacre in recent history with handguns: Virginia Tech. Neither have we forgotten that the 2nd Amendment exists for all law-abiding citizens, and giving up that right will only make the situation *worse* for these same law-abiding people and easier for criminals.

We truly understand that in a world where guns exist and criminals seem to have no problem getting hold of them, the last thing we should be doing is disarming ourselves under some fatalistic pretext that tells us that doing so will make the world a safer place. History disproves that *repeatedly*. It would be great to believe that politicians really do have our best interests at heart. It's just not so.

That is too difficult to believe because while we hear their denials, we see what they are trying to accomplish. Instead of putting armed guards at schools, these same politicians laugh at the idea when it is

---

[17] http://thehill.com/blogs/blog-briefing-room/news/290791-obama-shame-on-us-if-weve-forgotten-newtown#ixzz2OtAWFdDa (03/28/2013)

suggested by Wayne LaPierre of the NRA. Yet it turns out that armed guards have been suggested in the past and Clinton had a program that paid for armed guards to be placed in many schools across the nation. By 2007, funding for the program was beginning to dry up, and by 2009 Obama was the one who canceled the funding for that program altogether.[18] The point really is that when Clinton created this program – *COPS in Schools* – in 1999, the politically correct left did *not* laugh. They apparently thought it was a great idea because it was funded.

However, with the program essentially *not* in place at the time of several gun-related massacres, including Sandy Hook, the left found time to laugh because the armed guards in school suggestion came from those who are not considered part of the politically correct left. It came from the NRA.

But what the politically correct dutifully *avoid* is presenting facts that do harm to their line of "reasoning." *"According to the FBI, Americans use firearms in self-defense 2.1 million times annually. Cases where firearms are used criminally amount to 579,000. Seventy percent of those cases are carried out by criminal repeat offenders."*[19]

Moreover, according to a 1992 study by the FBI, *"violent crime rates are highest overall in states with laws severely limiting or prohibiting the carrying of concealed firearms for self-defense."*[20] Of course, this factual information does not support the politically correct agenda and in fact squarely *negates* it. Other statistics state the following:

- *In the vast majority of those self-defense cases, the citizen will only brandish the gun or fire a warning shot.*

---

[18] http://sistertoldjah.com/archives/2012/12/22/where-was-the-liberal-outrage-over-clintons-cops-in-school-federal-grant-program/ (03/28/2013)

[19] http://www.redstate.com/dloesch/2013/03/28/piers-morgan-admits-truth-behind-magazine-restrictions/ (03/29/2013)

[20] http://www.kc3.com/CCDW_Stats/fla_model.htm (03/29/2013)

- *In less than 8% of those self-defense cases will the citizen even wound his attacker.*
- *Over 1.9 million of those self-defense cases involve **handguns**.*
- *As many as 500,000 of those self-defense cases occur away from home.*
- ***Almost 10% of those self-defense cases are women defending themselves against sexual assault or abuse.*** [21]

In spite of these clear statistics, those within the politically correct camp do whatever they can to ignore the plain facts of the matter. That they do this simply proves their actual agenda, not their stated one. While they may push for the elimination of high-capacity magazines, it is clear that their real focus is on eliminating magazines that hold even one bullet.

Those within politically correct circles do what they can to restrict the 2nd Amendment, in spite of the built-in admonishment against it. In one case, an Alabama state Democrat by the name of Joe Mitchell responded tersely (and racially) to a resident named Eddie Maxwell who had written him asking that he not introduce new gun control legislation. The response from Mitchell is certainly cause for concern.

"Hey man. You have used the word 'except' when I think you mean somethin' else.

"Hey man. Your folk never used all this sheit (sic) to protect my folk from your slave-holding, murdering, adulterous, baby-raping, incestuous, snaggle-toothed, backward-a**ed, inbreed, imported criminal-minded kin folk. You can keep sending me stuff like you have however because it helps me explain to my constituents why they should protect

---

[21] http://www.redstate.com/dloesch/2013/03/28/piers-morgan-admits-truth-behind-magazine-restrictions/ (03/29/2013; emphasis in original)

that 2nd amendment thing AFTER we finish stocking up on spare parts, munitions and the like.

"Bring it. As one of my friends in the Alabama Senate suggested – 'BRING IT!!!!'" [22]

Ultimately, regardless of what they publicly state, anti-gunners (the politically correct left) want to ban guns in society. This is their goal and they will use whatever tactics they can to shame, embarrass, and blame, all the while stating that they support the 2nd Amendment. Do they? Of course not, and it is obvious to anyone who is not part of the politically correct subculture.

Rep. Joseph Mitchell is black and Eddie Maxwell is white. I'm wondering, though, how Mitchell knew that in order to respond to him the way he did. There is great concern today about our elected officials and the tendency of many of them to think that certain amendments can be set aside. This appears to be the reason why Maxwell wrote his letter in the first place, only to receive the racist rejoinder from Mitchell. It flies in the face of courtesy, but under the unwritten rules of politically correct engagement, since Mitchell is black, what he says and does is accepted (though with consternation) because of the *past*. In other words, he's a "victim" and allowed certain postures.

Apparently, in his full-blown racist torrent, Mitchell believes that since *some* white people were/are racist, this entitles him to be racist toward *all whites*. This type of attitude has no place in the halls of any political arena, but we are seeing it all too often, thanks to political correctness.

If our elected officials actually cared about the young people who are dying in big cities and truly wanted to save lives, they would not

---

[22] http://redalertpolitics.com/2013/03/28/alabama-democratic-legislator-calls-gun-advocates-ancestors-baby-raping-and-snaggle-toothed/ (04/04/2013)

want to limit or disarm law-abiding citizens. In fact, they would make every effort to create *safe* schools, which by their very nature cannot be "gun free" killing zones.

But while politicians are too often telling us that they have no intention of taking guns from law-abiding citizens, it appears that this is, at least at times, a lie. In May 2013, after a Senate Budget and Appropriations Committee hearing had just concluded, several Democrat senators continued to talk about gun control legislation. Without realizing their words were being recorded, they had a brief conversation.

> *"We needed a bill that was going to confiscate, confiscate, confiscate."*

> *"They don't care about the bad guys. All they want to do is have their little guns and do whatever they want with them."*[23]

The conversation is between Senator Loretta Weinberg (D37), Senator Sandra Cunningham (D31), Senator Linda Greenstein (D14), and at least one staff member. In spite of what the public is told by Democrats, it would appear that what we're told is not always the truth. Lying appears to be something that is perfectly acceptable within the construct of politics as well as political correctness.

What these Democrats fail to understand is that more gun control laws does not equate to less crime, even though many people believe that this is the case. It's simply not true and I have written several articles about this for my own blog[24] as well as The Brenner Brief,[25] for which I contribute articles.

---

[23] http://www.examiner.com/article/open-mike-reveals-n-j-senators-contempt-for-gun-owners-confiscation-goal (05/15/2013)
[24] http://www.studygrowknowblog.com
[25] http://www.thebrennerbrief.com

We can no sooner take guns away from criminals than we can win the war on drugs. There are too many guns available in society to address any problems related to that fact by attempting to remove guns. People should have the continued right whether they will choose to keep and bear arms or not. It is a guaranteed right given to us by the Constitution and it is clear that too many politicians these days resent the fact that they cannot simply take away that right, along with others.

Too many politicians on the left want to micro-manage society and they have already gotten away with too much as it is now. As they continue to chip away at the freedoms we enjoy, the noose tightens around our necks. That is the end result of the subversive nature of political correctness.

The politically correct subculture apparently believes that they need to take care of you by limiting what you can say, do, and buy. If this doesn't smack of George Orwell's "1984" to you, then unfortunately, nothing likely will.

Chapter 4

Politically Correct Intimidation

There are several ways that those within the politically correct left get their message across to the world. They lie, for one thing, as I've mentioned. The politically correct have no problem lying because they believe the end justifies the means. As long as they ultimately get what they want, lying serves their purposes.

The politically correct also attack. This is done normally in a very emotional and verbal way. At times, it has moved into the area of physical confrontations as well. A case in point is highlighted by the protests surrounding the recently heard arguments by the Supreme Court of the United States regarding same-sex marriage. At one point, an altercation broke out between the *National Organization for*

Marriage (NOM) and gay marriage advocate (and former Occupy Member) Sergei Kostin, who is said to have thrown the first punch.[26]

Ultimately, the intent of the politically correct left is to silence any opposing viewpoint. They're not interested in hearing it and they obviously believe that anyone who disagrees with them should be verbally assaulted into silence. In other words, the 1st Amendment should not apply to those they deem "haters." This is never more clearly seen as it is in the area of same-sex unions.

But what we do not see is what takes place beyond our sight, in the gay bars throughout America, where hatred is ramped up as far as it can go to incite weak-willed individuals to do what the law prohibits. Kevin Dujan (who happens to be gay and conservative) spends a good amount of time on his HillBuzz blog highlighting these types of happenings and events within the gay community. As a conservative, he is completely opposed to the things they do to drive their point home. Yet, he's gay, so I suppose it would be ridiculous to accuse him of being a "gay-hater," wouldn't it?

Dujan contrasts conservatives with the left. *"Unlike conservatives, who are more or less focused on peacefully living their own lives and generally react to events instead of setting them in motion, the political Left in this country feverishly works every day to proactively cause things to happen in the national conversation that will either benefit the Left politically or cause great harm to their perceived 'enemies'."*[27]

His point is clear. We conservatives are generally content to live our lives and let others live theirs. Yes, we have opinions and we're not afraid to voice them when the need arises, but in general, we appre-

---

[26] http://weaselzippers.us/2013/03/27/professional-activist-pushing-for-gay-marriage-attacks-traditional-marriage-advocate-outside-supreme-court/ (03/27/2013)
[27] http://hillbuzz.org/how-gay-community-leaders-promote-hate-and-encourage-violence-against-christians-chicagos-sidetrack-the-video-bar-as-case-study-53243 (03/27/2013)

ciate and enjoy life and prefer to live in peace. The politically correct left are not like that at all. They do whatever they can to agitate things. They are not content to simply leave things alone, but must be actively engaged in opposing anyone who has a differing opinion, whether it's related to same-sex marriage or something else.

Dujan goes on to discuss what happens too often in many gay bars throughout this nation. Since Kevin is gay, he should know. Further, from his own blog's "About Us" page, we learn that *"he's a conservative, Christian gay man residing in the rainbow-tinted neighborhood of Chicago known as 'Boystown,' where he writes, researches, and edits from this Buzzquarters command center."*[28]

Regarding politically correct gays and what they advocate in gay bars, Dujan notes, *"Sidetrack [a gay bar], for years, has been the mecca of anti-Christian hatred in Chicago's gay community. Any and all events the bar holds — but particularly those held for Equality Illinois — metastasize into Orwellian 'two-minute-hates' against Christians and Republicans."*[29]

Is it any wonder that someone like Floyd Corkins II finally breaks down and hides a gun in a Chick-Fil-A bag and then heads on over to Family Research Center with intent to kill? Interestingly enough, as Dujan points out, Corkins worked at *"the DC Center, an LGBTQAI community center in the nation's capital."*[30]

There is a photo on Dujan's website that highlights *"Chicago public school teacher...Bradley Thomas Balof [as he] incites a crowd of gay men to hurl expletives at Christians and Republicans in the form of a Chick-Fil-A effigy during a two-minute-hate conducted during a fund-*

---

[28] http://hillbuzz.org/contact-us-faq/about-kevin-dujan (03/26/2013)
[29] http://hillbuzz.org/how-gay-community-leaders-promote-hate-and-encourage-violence-against-christians-chicagos-sidetrack-the-video-bar-as-case-study-53243 (03/27/2013)
[30] Ibid

raiser for Equality Illinois held at Sidetrack the Video Bar in Chicago in August 2012."[31]

I have to appreciate what Dujan says about this event and the individuals who consider themselves to be "liberal." Dujan states, with a bit of irony, *"If you still use the word 'liberals' to describe these people, please stop, because there is nothing 'liberal' about hate mongering and inciting people to violence like this. This behavior is positively Islamic, not 'liberal', in its chanting and crowd-riling."*[32]

The saddest part of the above statement has to do with the numbers of so-called Christians who support (and even join with) these types of individuals who are so filled with hatred that they believe they can use whatever means available to them to squash the opposition. Remember, with political correctness, there are only two categories of people: those who are determined to be the "victim" and those who are seen as the "oppressors." While *all* mercy is extended to "victims," none is given to the "oppressors."

Of course, since most of us do not go to gay bars (or regular bars, for that matter), we are not acquainted with what goes on there. Who knew that these types of antics took place out of eyesight of the rest of America?

Dujan warns us about the fact that these events and attitudes do not take place at a bar called Sidetrack, in Chicago, as an anomaly. According to him, events like these occur all over America. *"There is a bar like Sidetrack in every major city doing the exact same thing to pump gay people up to commit acts of violence against Christians, conservatives, and anyone else deemed an 'enemy of the gay community'. The media just won't report on it, largely for the exact same reason*

---

[31] http://hillbuzz.org/how-gay-community-leaders-promote-hate-and-encourage-violence-against-christians-chicagos-sidetrack-the-video-bar-as-case-study-53243 (03/27/2013)
[32] Ibid

they also refuse to report on all of the hate mongering and violence en-couraging that occurs regularly in mosques of 'the religion of peace' that is Islam. **It doesn't suit the Left's agenda** *for its media opera-tives to inform you of the 'two minute hates' that indoctrinate the Left's goon squads in public places frequented by the gay community.*"[33]

I've emphasized part of Dujan's last statement about why the media fails to report on these things. I believe he's correct that it does not fit the agenda of the left. But the reason we must determine is, why doesn't it fit the left's agenda? That reason has everything to do with the fact that those within the politically correct left lie as a matter of course. They do their best to project one thing while underneath and out of sight they do something else entirely.

Recently, the Obama administration was dealt several blows in the form of scandals. Benghazi came back to haunt the Obama admin-istration through whistle-blower testimony that undercut Obama's and the State Department's explanations. Beyond Benghazi, the world learned that the DOJ illegally and secretly gathered phone rec-ords of AP press. We also learned that the IRS targeted conservative groups applying for non-profit status, often providing them with more requirements and allowing their applications to languish for months or even more than a year.

This is a form of intimidation that, at this point, may have a connec-tion to the White House. The IRS specifically targeted groups that had "tea party" or "patriot" in their names. They even went after several ministries that have been around for decades, like the Billy Graham Association. Beyond this, apparently, the IRS illegally shared infor-mation from some applications with a left-leaning group called ProPublica.

---

[33] http://hillbuzz.org/how-gay-community-leaders-promote-hate-and-encourage-violence-against-christians-chicagos-sidetrack-the-video-bar-as-case-study-53243 (03/27/2013)

All of this makes one wonder just exactly what is going on deep within the bowels of our government. How can people be this corrupt and think they won't eventually get caught?

Only a few short weeks prior to these scandals coming to the surface, Obama spoke at a college graduation. There he warned students to "reject these voices that warn of big government and tyranny,"[34] yet these scandals prove that our government is involved in tyranny against Americans.

If the average person (even among the left) knew what was going on in the shadows, he might be appalled to learn just how pervasive things have become in our government and throughout society. For this reason, the politically correct left needs desperately to hide their true agenda from the American public.

The PC collective of America (and the world) cannot admit that Islam is not a religion of peace. It cannot recognize that there are terribly harsh people in the various communities they seek to protect. They must cover up the fact that within large portions of the gay community, the unadulterated hatred toward Christians and conservatives in general is always on display and is ignored.

This same PC collective cannot admit the fallacies about their gun-control position or that racism toward whites is at an all-time high. These are the sacred cows to the politically correct that must be protected at all costs.

These are the things that drive their movement, and without them they would lack motivation. The truth of the matter is found in the fact that for the politically correct, traditional values must be purged from society.

---

[34] http://www.theblaze.com/stories/2013/05/05/obama-to-college-students-reject-these-voices-that-warn-of-big-government-tyranny/ (05/15/2013)

Political correctness, which has come to undergird society (which ushers in Cultural Marxism), is the downfall of America. More importantly, it is the great human revolt against God and His truth.

As one blogger recently noted, this is exactly what the politically correct left want – the *exile* of Christians and anything that smacks of values that are based on the Bible.[35]

Paul tells us in Romans 1:24, "*Therefore God gave them over in the lusts of their hearts to impurity, so that their bodies would be dishonored among them.*"

No matter how many times history repeats itself, there seems to always be a new generation ready to go down that same road of mistakes.

Woe to those so-called Christians who join in with them.

---

[35] http://wyblog.us/blog/religion/gay-marriage-is-christian-persecution.html (03/27/2013)

Chapter 5

Politically Correct Reverse Racism

W hen it all comes down to it, *political correctness* is an out and out attack on anything that smacks of what the left believes is of the white Christian male value system and the position derived from it. Those within politically correct circles will attack that position without mercy. What this means is that ultimately, the attack is against white men who are believed to be part of (and who created) the "good ol' boy" system that is seen as keeping women and minorities down.

However, anyone who agrees with and supports the perceived white male position is also attacked, though it is interesting how the left attacks. For instance, white people who are part of the politically correct left would never come out and condemn white males unless they did it as someone who supports the "victim."

From this vantage point, it becomes acceptable to bash white men because they are seen as the "aggressors" who have come together for the purpose of keeping everyone else from gaining their piece of the American pie. Because of this, it is perfectly acceptable to harbor and use racist and sexist attitudes toward white men because white men are seen as *the* problem, the main oppressor.

This is probably most clearly seen as Thomas Sowell points out in his book *Dismantling America*. He references a black student who responded to the arrests in the Duke Rape case, in which several white males were arrested on the testimony of a black stripper who accused them of raping her. The young black male (from North Carolina Central University) *"wanted to see the Duke students prosecuted, 'whether it happened or not. It would be justice for things that happened in the past'."*[36] Sowell referred to that demeanor as an "ugly attitude" that did its part to create a pall over the entire situation.

The case eventually lost steam because of the lack of credibility of the stripper and her own friends who came forward as witnesses *against* her. Her lack of credibility was not based on the fact that she was a stripper, but because of some of the things she told her friends and the fact that she lied. Still, it shows that at least some believed these young white male students of privilege at Duke should be taken down a notch or two whether they were guilty or not, simply to create a perceived form of "equality" and "justice." Of course, if the men were innocent and found guilty, then justice would not have been served at all.

This sort of perceived "equality" has no justice attached to it and therefore it does not create equality at all, but *injustice.* Those Duke

---

[36] Thomas Sowell *Dismantling America* (2010), p. 306

students could no more help being born into families that obviously could afford to send their sons to a school like Duke any more than I was born into a family that could *not,* and we're both *white*. This is the unparalleled tragedy that drives political correctness. It is not at all interested in pursuing justice as much as it is interested in pursuing a form of equality that leaves justice far behind. It's a tit for tat mentality and nothing more.

It is the way political correctness forms opinions about important issues. It does so by lining up people involved and separating the "victim" from the "aggressor" and moving from that vantage point in an effort to "solve" the problem. But since decisions are based not on some absolute truth but a moveable, ever-changing truth, the rules are constantly changing. Ultimately, it is generally agreed on by everyone within politically correct circles that the white male is the *main* "aggressor." The rest within society are constantly jockeying for position to see who will be the biggest "victim" of the moment. That normally goes to the black male, although that can be a variable depending upon the situation.

For instance, in Atlanta Public Schools, a cheating scandal was uncovered that allegedly occurred when former Superintendent Beverly Hall oversaw the district. To date, 35 employees – all black – within the district ranging from teachers, to administrators, to others (including Hall) have been indicted because of it. Apparently, the worst part of the whole thing is not the cheating itself (though that is bad enough). It is the racketeering charges stemming from the financial bonuses educators received because of the higher test scores.

Parents are understandably upset, as are other educators in the same school district who were *not* involved in this scandal. But the real question is, what will the outcome be? According to one editorial in the *Atlanta Journal-Constitution*, the fault is primarily due to the No Child Left Behind Act (NCLB), which was instituted during the Bush administration and which required state accountability for student achievement to the federal government. The growing sentiment seems to be that the cheating was caused by inappropriate achievement standards for all students, including students of low socioeconomic status. The editorial essentially states that NCLB has cheated students out of a real education because the schools became test-prep centers. The achievement targets ultimately led to educators "having" to cheat because the targets were unattainable.

So, one wonders then, because the overwhelming majority of students (and educators) in the Atlanta Public Schools are black, will political correctness extend itself into this upcoming courtroom drama and eventually find that the undue pressure of NCLB is ultimately responsible for the reason these educators did what they did? Only time will tell.

As far as the white male being the "oppressor," it is amazing how often society finds a way to bash the white male because of that perception. I've lost track of how many commercials highlight the white male as a true idiot. He's a moron and if it were not for women and minorities, the white male would forget how to breathe. He obviously isn't smart enough to determine when he needs cough syrup. Instead of buying a great new cell phone with his tax return, he's more interested in buying the wrestling belt buckle. The white male has no ability to cook and when his wife says "jump," that white male is ready with "how high?" The white male is the essential butt of jokes because if you use the black man or another male person of color, you risk being accused of racism. Better to use a white male, and if the white male is offended, who cares?

The white male is believed to be *the* cause of racism, and turn-around is fair play. Obviously, in the early days of the United States, there were white males who were racist. Certainly, some of them exist today as well. But most minorities (including women) have far more power today than the white male ever does, but no one would admit that because it would prove they are not really interested in equality or freedom, but in attaining a greater level of influence in society than white males have now. Remember, equality yearns to treat all people equally, but in today's society, minorities receive special privileges due to perceived slights and attitudes of racism and bigotry that is alleged to come mainly from the white male. The goal is to overcome the alleged power of the white male and whether or not he truly has any is moot.

But of course, this is exactly why the politically correct can and do attack minorities and women when their position mirrors that of the white male – the "aggressor." It really all boils down to an attack on white men, and this has been going on for decades. The point has been to undermine the value of the white male in society because of the traditional value system that is connected to that white male from the founding of this country, found within Christianity.

Women and minorities who also understand what the politically correct left is about and who choose to stand their ground against the left's assault are treated the same way that white males are treated. We've talked about this before and more examples and information were provided in my previously published book, *Falling Away*.

But of course, even though the attacks on the white male have become more frequent and focused, the politically correct left would prefer to focus on issues rather than on a particular race. Focusing on specific issues allows the left to bypass the level of accusation that would come their way if all they did was denounce white men. So, those in the PC camp do their best to level their accusations and denouncements at the issues while tossing in some strong verbiage that is used to point out and emphasize the fact that these issues exist because they are embraced mainly by white males.

As Anthony Browne so aptly put it, "*Political correctness promotes the creation of the 'victim mentality', discourages people from taking re-*

sponsibility for their own lives, suppresses free speech, and distorts public debate, leading to bad polices being adopted."[37]

What we have seen since political correctness bounced onto the national scene is the creation of a victim class structure. People want desperately to be part of it because they believe they will be protected and receive government subsidies that they would not otherwise receive, simply because they *appear* to be a "victim."

Think of groups that are not to be criticized. Blacks. Muslims. Gays. Feminists. Liberals. Democrats. These groups have created an aura around them of being the victim and because of the politically correct mindset are allowed to benefit from society solely on that basis alone. Moreover, those who critique or question them or their motives are quickly seen as "aggressors." This type of mentality is what Browne refers to as striving for the bottom as opposed to reaching for the top.

In essence, they *do* wind up on top by going to the bottom. By constantly bemoaning their perceived disrespected state in society, they are given the attention they do not deserve but receive anyway because of how political correctness works.

The permeating attitude that has found its way through society is that people of color are poor and without privileges because they are minorities and for no other reason. Yet, could it have something to do with the fact that in some cases, people are poor because they are lazy? That's off-limits for discussion though because it is not politically correct, is it? Poor people are thought to be poor because they have not gained from "white privilege," which has kept them down.

Political correctness does not allow the question to be raised and if one ventures into that area, the automatic response from the politically correct crowd is that the person who asked the question is a

---

[37] Anthony Browne *The Retreat of Reason* (2006), p.42

racist (or sexist, or bigot). Surely, not everyone who is a minority and is poor is so because of that, are they? There must be a percentage of individuals who are poor because they prefer it since it allows them to receive subsidies from the government. There actually *are* people who would prefer to receive a handout (even if they can work) than have an actual job, aren't there? To believe that this is essentially a small amount of people is to fully ignore the obvious.

"In the U.S. the widespread use of historical slavery as an excuse for failure merely inculcates a defeatist sense of victimhood that may be emotionally comforting in the short term, but does nothing to help African-Americans take what steps they can to improve their own lives."[38]

We know that this is true, but it seems that those who believe and push their politically correct agenda do not care if blacks become better off or more impoverished. It happens because it all boils down to votes, and unfortunately, when the government hands out freebies, people who receive those freebies wind up becoming beholden to that same government.

This is certainly one of the ways that political correctness works. Not interested in maintaining the standards created by the rule of law in America (or elsewhere), PC leftists are more interested in gaining position and power by creating a loyal base, a base that knows or cares little for the Constitutional foundation for America's laws. What matters is getting what you want.

Politically correct leftists have been creating problems for people who have opinions opposed to theirs for quite some time. As I've pointed out, they deal with issues publicly, but in reality, they are opposed to Christians, Republicans, and conservatives in general. It

---

[38] Anthony Browne *The Retreat of Reason* (2006), p.47

has to do with biblical values – or at least traditional values – adhered to by those within these groups.

It's always interesting to hear how the politically correct fight against rights that are guaranteed by the Constitution or Bill of Rights. Usually, they'll take what they consider to be the high road by focusing on the safety of people. This is what they do when it comes to gun control. They must emphasize the fact that people are killed by guns throughout American society. But that is all that they emphasize. They deliberately fail to point out that people have used guns to save their lives or someone else's, and many times the people using these guns don't even have to fire a shot. This is something that the politically correct oddly leave out as if it has nothing to do with anything.

The truth of it is that people do use guns to kill people. Criminals use them during the commission of a violent crime. Law-abiding people use them to save themselves from harm when they run up against a criminal. People do die because guns exist.

People also die because people drink, then drive, and then wind up killing someone because of their stupidity. People die because of illegal drug use. People are killed with hammers, knives, and even fists every year, and do I need to point out that slightly fewer than 4,000 unborn children are murdered every day in America?

It is true that people die every day. No amount of laws will correct that. There are laws against driving and texting, yet people text all the time. Some of them even have accidents and in some of those accidents, people die.

There are laws against murder, stealing, prostitution, graft, lying while under oath, running a red light or stop sign, and a million other things to boot. Are they all obeyed all the time? Unfortunately they are not. People break the laws of this land on a daily basis. Sometimes it's done accidentally, while other times, laws are broken maliciously. The point is that people break laws and sometimes bad things happen because of that fact.

But the politically correct continue to force us to believe that by making more laws, things will be better. Unfortunately, the only laws they are interested in creating are those that work against the traditional laws of this land. No matter how "poignantly" they may argue their point that "guns kill people," it is simply a ruse on their part to curtail (or eliminate) the 2nd Amendment, in spite of how many times they regale us with their alleged loyalty to the Constitution.

Aren't you tired of our government making laws that have absolutely no effect on criminals, except for punishment? Laws do not stop criminals from doing what they do. These laws have no effect on them.

That will be the next argument coming from the politically correct. Because criminals do not obey laws, the only real course of action to take…(sigh)…is to ban all weapons throughout America. Yes, it's tragic that it has come to this (sigh) and it is a shame that criminals simply don't obey laws.

But, in order to save lives, we must take this extraordinary step and eliminate guns from society. It will still take a while, but good people understand why this is necessary and will comply. Those who don't will have to be punished because it's obvious they care more about themselves than the safety of society as a whole.

This type of tripe is nothing more than emotionally-laden garbage that is dredged up from the sewers of human experience and foisted upon society so that people will feel pushed into giving up their weapons and rights through guilt. It won't work. Intelligent people won't fall for it at all.

Of course, even if the government could eliminate guns from society, no one who has even a modicum of intelligence believes that criminals would no longer have them. The truth is that criminals would be the only ones who had them. Our government knows this, which simply proves that our government is not concerned about public safety at all. The government is concerned about the average person's ability to resist the government's illegal actions.

The same holds true where the 1st Amendment is concerned. We are starting to hear the rumblings in pockets of society that believe that free speech should be curtailed because people say things that others consider to be offensive. That's not a good enough reason. Every time I listen to Ed Schultz, Rachel Maddow, Chris Matthews, and others, I hear lies and offensive (even libelous) comments.

But the people who want to shore up our freedom of speech so that we would all live under limitations are not concerned about these people. The people who are concerned are only talking about conservatives who deign to have something to say that they don't like.

Whether the discussion is about gays or same-sex unions or Islam, the fact of the matter is that some people, motivated by political correctness, want to limit what Americans can say. This has already been done in the UK and is happening in Canada as well as other places.

Unfortunately for these countries, they neither have the 2nd Amendment or the 1st Amendment to contend with, so those governments can restrict the lives of people in what they say and with respect to the guns they can own. However, America does have these amendments and we conservatives take them seriously because we know that people died to create the conditions under which this country was founded. They are not merely guidelines or suggestions. They are law.

Yet we have another individual in America who is calling for a limitation on the 1st Amendment, at least on the Internet (for now). "*Dr.*

Qasim Rashid argued that cyber-bullying laws could be used to limit freedom of expression – such as the burning of Korans — in war time:

"*'When a nation is at war, many things that might be said in times of peace are a hindrance to this effort,' Rashid said on March 19 at Howard University. 'And their utterance will not be endured so long as men fight and...no court can regard them as protected by any constitutional right.'*"[39]

In essence, what Rashid is advocating is simple: replace the Constitutional 1st Amendment with Sharia law. He doesn't like it when people burn the Qur'an as a form of expression or protest.

It should come as no surprise that many Muslims living in the United States want to see Sharia law in our courtrooms. In fact, "*a coalition of faith groups met with Justice Department officials Monday to encourage the Obama administration to take a more public stance against anti-Muslim hate speech and hate crimes.*"[40]

Really? Yes, really. This happened way back in August of 2010. Muslims do not like the freedom that Americans have to disregard Sharia law in the name of freedom of speech and expression.

It's clear though that Muslims are mainly concerned about people offending Muslim sensibilities. That may or may not include offensive comments directed to or about Jesus, since He is a type of prophet for Muslims.

But in reality, when Muslims start to grumble about people saying or doing things that are offensive to Islam (like burning Qur'ans or drawing pictures of Muhammad), they want it to stop. They know they cannot stop it, so what they really want is a way to legally pun-

---

[39] http://creepingsharia.wordpress.com/2013/03/27/another-u-s-muslim-calls-for-limiting-americans-1st-amendment-rights-to-protect-islam/ (03/27-2013)
[40] http://creepingsharia.wordpress.com/2010/09/04/did-muslim-group-ask-doj-to-start-enforcing-sharia-blasphemy-law/ (03/27/2013)

ish those who offend Muslims through their speech or expression. If a law is passed (like the ones in the UK) barring people from making offensive statements, then there is a way to punish someone for making the offensive remark. Without a law in place, the only thing that Muslims can do is...get angry and protest. They do that enough as it is and the world seems to want to placate them because of it. However, Muslims want more, much more. They want Sharia law in place because every area of the world that caves to Sharia law becomes a place where Islam has gained a victory. All of these victories together lead to what they hope will be the next world Caliphate, where Islam will reign supreme. It doesn't matter that people are discriminated against because of it either.

If all this is not enough, another sort of discrimination is facing the people of Phoenix, AZ that stems from the notoriety given to affirmative action. Apparently, the city of Phoenix is willing to toss safety to the wind even if it means hiring lifeguards who are not good swimmers so that diversity needs will be met.[41] An article related to this issue states, "*Blacks, Latinos and Asians who may not necessarily qualify can still get hired, says the city official who adds that 'we will work with you in your swimming abilities'.*"[42]

The reason for this has to do with the number of minorities who use the public pools at 29 locations throughout Phoenix. The problem is not with them. The problem is seen as the fact that most of the current lifeguards are white. City officials say they simply "*don't like that*" because of language issues, etc. I would think knowing that a person is having a hard time in the water or drowning would be a universal language, not based on the difficulty someone might have articulating that in English.

---

[41] http://www.judicialwatch.org/blog/2013/04/city-recruits-minority-lifeguards-even-if-they-cant-swim/?utm_source=judicialwatch.org&utm_medium=twitter (04/03/2013)
[42] Ibid

The article goes onto say, *"Competitive swimming is a sport dominated by whites. In fact, studies have found that blacks and Hispanics have lower swimming proficiency compared to whites. In Phoenix public pool lifeguards have traditionally come from 'more affluent parts of town' where schools have swim teams. That means virtually no minorities, so the city launched this special program to recruit some.*

"Though this is a local effort in one city, it's also part of a national trend to boost the minority workforce at whatever cost. Under President Obama we have seen a lot of this at the federal level through a variety of specially-designed government programs that give ethnic minorities special treatment at all federal agencies as well as medical and agricultural fields, among others."[43]

This is the result of programs that cater to people based on ethnicity, all because of the perceived "white privilege" that many believe exists in society. The saddest part of this is that there are a plethora of low-income white kids who are completely bypassed because they are not a minority and their parents are not affluent. What about them? It doesn't seem to matter because of the perception that all white people cause racism, therefore minorities need to be catered to in order to balance the scales of equality and freedom.

If this discriminates against whites, does that matter? If the government endeavors to try to remove our 1st or 2nd Amendment rights, does that matter? It does not appear to be the case.

Maybe we need to start bean-counting with respect to how many athletes go to the Olympics who happen to be white, or how many NBA players happen to be black. Political correctness will gladly take us that far.

---

[43] http://www.judicialwatch.org/blog/2013/04/city-recruits-minority-lifeguards-even-if-they-cant-swim/?utm_source=judicialwatch.org&utm_medium=twitter (04/03/2013)

Chapter 6

Politically Correct Pecking Order

To hear some tell it, a girl who drinks too much and passes out is "asking for it." I'm referring to the rape case that occurred in the town of Steubenville, OH, in which two star athletes were put on trial and found guilty of rape. As expected, there are mixed reactions to the story.

What is a bit shocking is how much fervor there has been by those who support not the victim, but the young men, since the verdicts were handed down. In fact, it seems as though a good deal of support extends to one of the perpetrators specifically, Ma'lik Richmond. Could it have something to do with the fact that he is *black*? NAACP chapter president Mayo Royal believes that because Richmond is black, he got railroaded. The other perpetrator in the case – Trent Mays – is white and received two years in juvenile detention, compared with Richmond's one year. Who got railroaded?

Royal would have us believe that the evidence is severely lacking, but he seems to have his eyes wide shut. *"Trent Mays and Ma'lik Richmond were convicted of raping a 16-year-old girl on the night of Aug. 11, 2012. The two football players brought the victim to two separate parties as other teens photographed and documented the sexual abuse. The victim had been drinking heavily and was unconscious during the attacks. Videos and photos were shared by teens who attended the party, which would be later used as evidence against Mays, 17, and Richmond, 16."*[44]

NAACP chapter president Royal Mayo believes that the victim *"might have been a willing participant."*[45] Of course, if a white person said this about a black victim, we can only imagine the firestorm that would be ignited because of it. When you are thought to be the "victim" (as in a person of color), remember there is essentially nothing you can do or say that is considered wrong.

Because of the history of racism that you (or your race) may have experienced, you have permission to say things that others cannot get away with saying. Your status as victim allows you to make sexist (or simply revolting) statements and those statements do not make you appear to be a sexist (in this case).

You are simply speaking your mind based on your own past experience. In this case, the experience has to do largely with the alleged corruption within the Steubenville Police Department and its alleged racist profiling against minorities, specifically blacks.

---

[44] http://www.ibtimes.com/steubenvilles-naacp-president-says-rape-victim-was-drunk-willing-exclusive-1149517# (03/28/2013)
[45] Ibid

Certainly he has his reasons, but everything I've read about the incident (and Mayo's beliefs) is not persuasive enough to warrant a verdict of "innocent" or to have thrown the case out. The reality is that there was evidence, but that doesn't mean much when you are a person of color who simply doubts the official story and points to a number of circumstantial items to draw conclusions.

"Mays was videotaped digitally penetrating the victim. At a third party, the victim was unable to walk on her own, and, according to testimony, Richmond was seen digitally penetrating her from behind."[46]

Basically, the charge is that both defendants penetrated the victim with their *fingers.* If there is conclusive video/photographic evidence that shows what is alleged to have occurred between the rape victim and the perpetrators, you would think that would go a long way in convincing most that something illicit and illegal occurred. For many, that is simply not good enough.

Royal Mayo asks the question about immunity that he believes may have been part of the picture and answers the question as to why no one else was arrested. *"If none of these guys had immunity from the beginning and one of them made a pornographic movie with his phone with two teenagers, the other two admitted to taking pornographic photos or nude photos of the girl, if they had no immunity or no deal with the prosecutors or police, how come they are not under arrest?"*[47]

Mayo's point is that these guys allegedly broke the law by videotaping a crime instead of intervening to keep it from happening. The point is well-taken, but it still does not absolve the two defendants in the case. It seems more like Mayo simply wants as many people as possible to be arrested. The fact that they haven't been makes him believe that either a deal was done that included immunity or his

---

[46] http://www.ibtimes.com/steubenvilles-naacp-president-says-rape-victim-was-drunk-willing-exclusive-1149517# (03/28/2013)
[47] Ibid

point is simply voiced to add fuel to the fire that the whole situation is very unfair.

The prosecutor emphatically denied that anyone was given any immunity and that the investigation is still ongoing. This type of response does not satisfy people like Mayo and so he presses onward, convinced that cronyism, police corruption, and the always-present racism played a hand in the situation.

Of course, it goes without saying that Mayo's concern is only for Richmond, the lone black defendant. This brings up the question of whether or not people like Mayo would even be involved in this case if both perpetrators were white. After all, a group that reaches out to protect and ensure that white males have all the necessary resources at their disposal simply does not exist. When it does, the group that is reaching out is considered to be racist. Then again, the "victim" here (the black defendant because he has been categorized as a victim by the politically correct) always operates under the assumption that since he is not white, he does not benefit from white privilege.

White privilege – advanced by critical race theorists – is believed to automatically benefit those of the white race solely because they are white.[48] It's one of those things that cannot be proven, but it sounds plausible to minorities, therefore that is enough to secure it as a viable force to be reckoned with by those who are not white.

The politically correct have done a number on justice. They seek equality and freedom, but only for those considered to be victims.

But what about the real victim in this case, not the imagined ones who we refer to as "defendants"? What would Mayo's involvement in this situation be if the victim had been black? At this point, we do not know the victim's race or her name because she is only 16 years old. Unfortunately, because of the way things work, we can likely safely

---

[48] See the author's book *Falling Away* for more on this subject.

conclude that the young woman is not black, but likely white (or maybe "white-Hispanic?").

If you are black, according to the unwritten laws of political correctness, you are a victim solely because of your race. Due to this, when something "bad" happens to you, you still retain the label "victim." It doesn't matter whether you brought the situation on yourself or not. Black defendant Ma'lik Richmond is a case in point.

There was obviously enough evidence to secure a conviction of rape against him (along with co-defendant, Trent Mays, a young white male) and Richmond also tearfully apologized to the victim in court. Yet, because he had good grades and was a star athlete and black, many feel sad for him. They blame the young victim who some, like NAACP chapter president Royal Mayo, say was "asking for it." The assumption here is that either her words, actions, or both were sending out signals telling young men that she was sexually available and they should take advantage of that fact.

This harkens back to the days when "boys will be boys" and so what if they took advantage of some young girl? They're football *players* and that's what they are expected to do. These are "jocks" that train hard and play hard and most would agree that they are the popular young men in school, just as the cheerleaders are the popular young women. For these groups, special treatment is what they are used to receiving because of their role in high school.

I am glad that the investigation is continuing because from everything I have read, it appears that other laws were broken and people need to be held responsible. Where were the adults at these parties? How did alcohol become involved in the first place where underage people were gathered? Who brought it?

Some might consider that to be a superfluous question given the fact that for decades, when youth gather for parties, alcohol seems to flow freely. Another question is why some of these young people took photos or video of the crimes instead of trying to stop them from happening.

These are all good questions, but they are also – in my opinion – secondary to the primary question of whether or not the defendants did take advantage of a young female victim who – because of her drunkenness – was unable to protect herself from her attackers. This, by far, is the most important question. The others should be dealt with and hopefully will be in time.

But regarding the rape of the young woman, the whole situation is beyond absurd. I have read nothing from any women's group that stepped up to defend the young victim. They're pretty quick to stand behind someone like Sandra Fluke, though, who wants to have her contraceptives provided by the taxpayer.

If support from a women's group is there anywhere, I was unable to find anything at all. What I did find was a flurry of harassment, threats, and vile comments directed to the young victim and her family. A day after the verdict was handed down, two girls were arrested and charged with making on-line threats to the accuser (the real victim in this case).

To be sure, unfortunately, the Steubenville case does not stand alone. Not long after the Steubenville case, we see another case developing, this time in Torrington, CT, but it still involves football players. Four have been arrested in a case that involves rape. However, the victim in this case is only 13 years old.

"Two Torrington High School football players stand accused of sexual assault of a 13-year-old girl. Four others were suspended in a hazing scandal last fall that is still under investigation. One player, the team's second-highest scorer last fall, was allowed to play even though the

team's coach knew he had been charged with felony robbery and assault."[49]

At least one of the alleged perpetrators has a criminal history but was allowed to continue to be on the football team in spite of that. The message is clear. When you're an athlete, you're given special privileges that the law normally does not allow because of what you bring to the school.

But what is the most troubling part of this picture aside from the rape itself? The fact that many students posted comments on their social network page that condemned the 13-year-old girl, as if the fault lies with her. It is amazing that young people today can place blame where it does not belong largely because of their world view, which we know has been forever changed because of the political correctness that has gained such inroads into society.

Why is that happening? I believe it's happening because of several reasons. First of all, the students at the school probably like the two football players, and because of that they simply see the young girl who was raped as ruining their lives. She should not have gotten drunk. She shouldn't have passed out. She shouldn't have been available for the two jocks to fondle and penetrate. She should have made it impossible for them to disrobe her. That places the blame squarely on the shoulders of the young victim. Yes, she should have made better decisions. She should not have gotten drunk and it's too bad she passed out. However, does this mean that because two young men took advantage of her, it's her fault? That is ridiculous thinking, yet this is what at least some people believe to be the case, which is why we are hearing sentiments like "she got what she deserved" or "she asked for it." The young men should have made bet-

---

[49] http://www.registercitizen.com/articles/2013/03/20/news/
doc51493e14b1a0a944806262.txt

ter decisions as well. The fact that they did not is not the fault of the young girl.

But secondly, this type of reactionary stance to this tragedy exists because there is a pecking order within the politically correct arena of "victims" that comes into play here. In America, if you are *black*, you are essentially at the top of that pecking order. Other minorities (including women) come after that. At the same time, any and *all* of those "victims" are on equal footing when they stand against white (Christian) males.

What this means is very simple. Even though women are considered "victims," they are only truly victims when compared to white (Christian) males. In fact, that's how a victim is determined: by comparing them with white (Christian) males. So everyone other than white (Christian) males can be a victim of racial or sexual injustice or bigotry.

The difficulty, though, occurs when two individuals – both carrying the "victim" status – are up against one another. At that point, how do we choose the "real" victim? We need to remember that being black trumps all other "victims," even in a case when there has been a true victim of rape, as we've just seen.

In this case, the young woman is likely white (though of course, we cannot be certain). Therefore, even though women in general have "victim" status, when compared and contrasted with blacks (even black men), blacks are seen as the greater "victim" and therefore they will receive more societal sympathy because of it.

If the young victim is black, there is a likelihood that sympathy still would have gone to the young black man (not the white one). But criticism of the young victim then would not have been as severe.

There is a true pecking order within the overall system of "victims" as recognized by the politically correct left. It is a nuanced system, in which certain victims always maintain a greater status of victimhood than others.

Because blacks are considered to be the greatest victims in America – all because of the slavery issue – no one can trump them. When push comes to shove – black women against black men – the black man is still the greater victim. The only situation in which this is not true is in a situation where the black man is understood to be a conservative (as in the case of Anita Hill vs. Clarence Thomas). To make matters worse, Thomas is married to a white woman, which some in the black community see as an attempt to throw off one's blackness.

Political correctness is a true scourge on society. It can do nothing except bring society down, and this is exactly what is has done.

As I've said before, anything good that might have come from politically correct thinking has long been overthrown by the fact that its negatives far outweigh any positives associated with it. The emphasis in society should not be equality or freedom as political correctness tends to stress. The emphasis should be on justice for every person, period.

Justice – true justice – simply gives to each person what he or she has earned and it is not based on skin color, creed, or religious framework. It is based solely on the actions of each person. So Trent Mays and Ma'lik Richmond have been found guilty of raping a young woman. Because of that, they will spend time in custody. Is that justice? Yes, if they actually did the crime.

What about the young victim here? Is she receiving justice? Only as far as some people are concerned. Others want to excoriate her for what they consider to be her egregious actions that brought the rape on herself. They believe she should be held responsible for leading the young men on. It annoys me that women's groups especially do not see the double standard here, which is what they have spent years fighting against. Why is it fine to castigate this young female victim for making wrong decisions, but when the young men make wrong decisions that are criminal offenses toward another person, they are excused with the blame placed squarely at the feet of the female victim? How is this just?

Let's take a brief look at a situation that many of us are familiar with from the Bible to see how it played out. It involves David and Bathsheba, and maybe we will see some connections to today.

In 2 Samuel 11, the narrative explains how David – being bored and unable to sleep – went outside onto the roof of the palace. Lo and behold, as he surveyed the city of Jerusalem, he saw a woman – Bathsheba – bathing on the roof of her home.

So he did what any number of men might do – he sent for her and had her brought to him. Hey, he was the king. It was his right to commit adultery with any woman in his kingdom, right? Wrong. Bathsheba was married to one of David's true military warriors by the name of Uriah (the Hittite). To keep Uriah from finding out, David had Uriah killed in battle by having other men pull away from him.

Would people argue that Bathsheba should not have been bathing on the roof of her home? Would they accuse Bathsheba of "asking for it"? I hope not.

It was night and she bathed on the roof of her home out of sight of prying eyes. It was not her fault that the palace of David sat at the highest point in Jerusalem, allowing him to look over the rooftops of all the homes. It was also not her fault that instead of being out with his armies, leading them into battle, David had decided to remain at home in comfort. He got bored and he found trouble.

Did Trent Mays and Ma'lik Richmond have to go to that party? Did they have to respond to temptation that night? Did they have to use their fingers to penetrate a young girl of 16 after she had passed out? That's ridiculous, yet that is what some people think.

The principle at work here is that if opportunity rears its ugly head, even though that opportunity is illegal, a person cannot be blamed for taking advantage of the situation. This is not true and it is how humanistic relativism (which is certainly part of politically correct attitudes today) works in society.

This is why God's absolute truth is what it is and why it does not change depending upon the situation. His truth stands as the litmus test for what is the right and wrong way to react to the many situations that face us every day in our lives and in society.

It seems like a lot of things went wrong to create situations in which young people were forced to make decisions that have affected their lives. Whether it was simply attending a party where alcohol was available or raping a young woman who had too much of that alcohol, the whole premise was wrong. It created one situation after another where it became easy to do what was wrong in favor of how a person felt that night.

It is easy to blame others for the mistakes we make, isn't it? David originally did this but eventually admitted his fault and God told him what would happen because of it. The consequences of David's selfish, thoughtless, and even criminal actions were not to be avoided. They fell, as God said they would.

The two young football players have experienced something in their lives that has forever changed them. It's not the fact that they were found guilty of something. It's the fact that they both did something that was criminal and justice demands punishment.

The two young men and their supporters likely want the situation to go away. They would probably like to be let off with a warning. Is that justice? At least David had the integrity to fully admit his failures and understood that the consequences were right because of what he had set in motion.

What these young men and their supporters want is not justice. It is the demands of political correctness in action: seeking "equality," not justice.

Chapter 7
Politically Correct Justice

As mentioned, political correctness emphasizes equality and freedom to the exclusion (and detriment) of justice. This, in and of itself, creates a tenuous situation for people throughout society, depending upon their conceived status as either victims or aggressors. Those who are classified as aggressors are consequently blamed for the fact that victims exist at all.

In essence then, when we hear words like "equality" and "freedom" thrown about, we need to understand that these terms apply almost exclusively to those who are considered to be victims. That is the problem because those thought to be aggressors are immediately eliminated from being in order to gain equality or freedom. It is understood that the victims are trying to gain the same type of equality and freedom that aggressors allegedly already enjoy.

Since aggressors are thought to be the problem – the reason why victims exist at all – then of course the struggle is to gain equality and freedom for those who are victims due to the aggression of the oppressors. This, it is believed, will level the playing field. In truth, this is all some sort of belief system based on too many variables: variables that, while they may have some anchor in reality, cannot be empirically verified with finality by any quantitative means.

This is a stripped-down understanding of the way it works within the subculture of political correctness, and right now, the politically correct have the ear of society. Those who are not part of the politically correct hegemony have no real say in society because, as aggressors, they need to be shut down. This is exactly what the politically correct hope to achieve: the silencing of those who disagree with the tenets of political correctness.

Remember though, political correctness is simply the means by which change in a given society is created. It is not the end in and of itself. We need to be aware that this is how it works so that we do not get hung up on the process itself and lose focus.

Those within the politically correct culture are on the attack against the aggressor. They use the politically correct process to bring these issues to the surface so that the world can clearly see who the aggressors and the victims are throughout. Once it is visibly determined who comprises the two groups, the attack can begin on those who are seen as keeping victims in society at bay.

Instead of discussing justice, it is more important for those within the politically correct subculture of society to emphasize equality and freedom. First of all, this sounds much better because of the implications of both of these words. To work toward equality and freedom implies that a person or group is not equal and therefore is being held down, usually by someone else.

Justice itself too often has judicial or even criminal ramifications. When we think of justice, we conjure up courtroom scenes, with lawyers, prosecutors, and judges. Of course, justice is something that can actually be measured, whereas neither equality nor freedom can be. Maybe that's why political correctness emphasizes these two traits as opposed to something empirically-based like justice.

Let's not forget that the definitions of freedom and equality can mean something different for each group or person. Justice, on the other hand, has a definition that tends to apply itself to all circumstances and situations. Freedom and equality can be relative, based on situations, and that is the problem.

For instance, the George Mason University's Mercatus Center recently released a study showing that North Dakota is the freest state in America as far as the economy and personal freedom. This is based on *"tax rates, government spending and debt, regulatory burdens, and state laws covering land use, union organizing, gun control, education choice and more."*[50]

If we can measure something empirically, we may be able to disprove the claims of those within the politically correct subculture. That's not easy to do when speaking of the more ethereal qualities like equality and freedom.

Yet the politically correct movement marshals onward, seemingly oblivious to the assault on reason and decency that results from it. In its effort to strive for something that cannot be adequately measured

---

[50] http://sayanythingblog.com/entry/study-finds-north-dakota-is-the-freest-state-in-the-union/ (03/28/2013)

– equality and freedom – marks of inequality and restriction of freedom come into play in its wake.

So strongly do some believe in chasing equality and freedom that justice is actually denied in the process. Such is the case of the New
Black Panthers, two of whom stood outside a Philadelphia voting
precinct in an intimidating way that literally kept people from enter-
ing to vote. This occurred several years ago.

Though arrested, charged, and found guilty, their case was eventually
overturned by Attorney General Eric Holder's Department of Justice.
Why? No reason was given, but it certainly seems clear enough that
under Holder's DOJ, if you were black, you were given second and
even third chances though you had broken the law.

Some would argue that because of the level and amount of racism
that had gone on for generations against blacks (and, they argue, still
exists), this was simply a fair turn-around. But is that the way justice
works? No, it's the way equality and freedom can work.

Chapter 8

Politically Correct Jesus

One morning, as I scanned through one of the local papers for my area, I came across something that jumped out at me. It was an attempt to label Jesus as a liberal: a pluralistic liberal at that. The person believed that Jesus never judged and was the epitome of liberality when it came to dealing with the human race.

> *Webster's dictionary defines a Liberal as one who is open minded, not strict in the observance of orthodox, traditional or established forms or ways. Jesus was a pluralist Liberal who taught that one need not conform to strict and orthodox views of God, religion, and life. He rejected*

73

> *greed, violence, the glorification of power, the amassing*
> *of wealth without social balance, and the personal judg-*
> *ing of others, their lifestyles, or beliefs.*[51]

My first question is, *where do I begin* in my biblical refutation of these fallacious comments?

Let's start with the word "liberal" and Webster's definition of it. This *used* to be the definition of a "liberal," but unfortunately, liberals themselves have changed. Like most of society, the liberal person has been redefined by the insurgency of political correctness. That particular mindset has reimagined the liberal, as it were.

The liberal who *used* to be open-minded is no longer such. In fact, anyone with whom the liberal disagrees is routinely vilified. That is simply how political correctness has done its work. The label "liberal" is really a misnomer since the only open-mindedness the liberal embraces is for other individuals who think as he/she does. They are completely *closed-minded* with anyone who does not share their way of thinking.

As far as the liberal not being strict in observance with respect to traditional or orthodox ways and forms, that is certainly the truth. The liberal of today – while they at one time *respected* those who were strict in their observance of traditional ways – essentially rejects traditional values and orthodoxy and expects everyone else to reject them as well.

When the individual quoted begins talking about Jesus, it is clear that he or she either has no real working knowledge of the Bible or he or she sees things (as do most liberals) from an allegorical standpoint. To this type of person, the "moral" of the story is far more important than the actual incident itself or teaching that comes from it.

---

[51] The Henry County Times, March 27, 2013, p. 5 "Quips from You to Us"

Regarding the quote's inclusion of the term "pluralistic liberal," we should probably take a moment to define that. There have been many things written on the subject of liberal pluralism, but it is likely that William A. Galston is best known for the subject, or at least, *one* of the best known.

He states, with respect to liberalism, "*Liberalism requires a robust though rebuttable presumption in favor of individuals and groups leading their lives as they see fit, within a broad range of legitimate variation, in accordance with their own understanding of what gives life meaning and value. I call this presumption the principle of expressive liberty. This principle implies a corresponding presumption (also rebuttable) against external interference with individual and group endeavors.*"[52]

It is easy to see how this definition of "liberal" does not really define *today's* liberal as corrupted by political correctness. Today's liberal is not in favor of people living their lives as they see fit. Today's liberal believes that external interference with individuals and groups *should* play a part in the way our lives are lived today.

While it is difficult to succinctly phrase all the meanings of liberal pluralism, it might best be summed up thusly. Liberal pluralism essentially believes:

- Individual choice and freedom are seen as a crucial human right.
- Democratic societies allow a range of political views and opinions and a range of political parties between which the population chooses in free elections.

Based then on this information, the person quoted is saying that the historical figure of Jesus was a liberal pluralist in the sense that he understood that choice and freedom are a basic human right. Beyond

---

[52] William A. Glaston *Liberal Pluralism* (Cambridge Press, 2002), p. 3

this, he or she would argue that He also understood (and allowed for) a range of political views and opinions among the populace.

This is the starting point of the person quoted. This person has *assumed* that because *he or she* is a liberal pluralist, so is Jesus because of certain things he or she sees in His life. Unfortunately, I believe this person has taken exception to the Bible and stretched the truth beyond credulity.

According to the person quoted, the following characteristics apply to Jesus:

- taught that one need not conform to strict and orthodox views of God, religion, and life
- rejected greed, violence, the glorification of power, the amassing of wealth without social balance, and
- rejected the personal judging of others, their lifestyles, or beliefs

Let's look at each of these for a moment. Did Jesus teach that conformity to a strict and orthodox view of God, religion, and life was unnecessary? Not from where I sit.

In fact, throughout the gospels, we learn that Jesus came to fulfill the Law (of Moses), not destroy it. He clearly stated His intentions in Matthew 5:17 when He said, *"Do not think that I came to abolish the Law or the Prophets; I did not come to abolish but to fulfill."* This is, of course, simply one example of His absolute respect and devotion to the Law from the Hebrew Bible (the Old Testament).

If we consider that within the Mosaic Law, there existed 613 individual laws, that represents quite a list. While some of those laws were specific to the Levitical Priesthood, there were still hundreds of laws and regulations that the average Jewish person was expected to fulfill. Obviously, if Jesus is saying that He came to *fulfill* the Law, not abolish it, then He is also obviously conforming to strict and even orthodox views of religion, isn't He?

Jesus was even very careful about paying the Temple tax, though He was not really under any compunction to do so since He was the Messiah. Nonetheless, He tells Peter to go fishing and take the coin out of the fish's mouth that he was going to catch. That coin would cover the Temple tax for both Jesus and Peter. He did this so that the religious leaders would not be "offended" if He chose not to pay the tax. This is clear from Matthew 17:27 which tells us, "*However, so that we do not offend them, go to the sea and throw in a hook, and take the first fish that comes up; and when you open its mouth, you will find a shekel. Take that and give it to them for you and Me.*"

Jesus was extremely careful to fulfill *all* of the Law. He was strict regarding orthodoxy in religion and life.

What people (like the person quoted) fail to understand is that there is a tremendous difference between obedience to the Law and obedience to tradition. Obedience to the Law prohibited Jesus from doing certain things, of course. However, there was nothing in the Law that prohibited Him from speaking with a Samaritan woman in a public place (the well; cf. John 4). Jesus broke no Law by speaking with her and asking her for a drink of water.

What Jesus did was to strip away the tradition from the Law, fulfilling the Law, but in many cases ignoring the humanly-created tradition, which not only failed to add anything to God's Law, but more often than not, wound up *hiding* the truth of God's Law under mountains of tradition. This made the Law very confusing for the average Jewish person who earnestly wanted to follow the Law in order to please God.

Jesus stripped away layers of tradition so that the Law could stand on its own. Having done that, He fulfilled every bit of it. Paul tells us in

1 Corinthians 5:21, *"[God] made Him who knew no sin to be sin on our behalf, so that we might become the righteousness of God in Him."*

Of course Jesus rejected *greed, violence, glorification of power* and *the gathering to Himself of wealth* simply to be rich! Greed, violence (for violence's sake), chasing after power and riches – these are all *sins* and Jesus would have none of it!

But what I believe the person I've quoted misses is several cogent points here. Jesus refused the Tempter's musings in Matthew 4 when he tempted Jesus to bow down and worship him. In exchange, the Tempter would give Jesus all the kingdoms of the world. This was a short cut he offered to Jesus. In the end, Jesus *will* have the physical reign over the entire earth and will rule over all the kingdoms of this world. Jesus simply refused to do it Satan's way by avoiding the cross.

I'm not sure our liberal pluralist friend whom I've quoted truly understands that this is the reason Jesus rejected Satan's offer in the first place. Jesus would not avoid the cross. It was the reason He came into this world.

Jesus' rejection of violence as a means of gaining dominion over the world was in keeping with the Father's will. He went through this world peacefully, resisting the urge to react the way the world reacts. Why? Because He had to get to the cross.

Even in the Garden of Gethsemane on the night of His betrayal, He rebuked Peter for cutting off the ear of the centurion guard and told Peter that even now, if Jesus chose, He could call on His Father to send legions of angels to rescue Him. He goes on to ask how the Scriptures would be fulfilled if He chose that path (cf. Matthew 26:47-55).

As far as rejecting wealth without the balance of social responsibility, the person I've quoted may be referring to the rich young ruler of

Mark 10:17-27. Here, we learn that this young man comes to Jesus and asks what he should do to be saved. Jesus points out that he needs to sell everything he has, give to the poor, and follow Jesus. The man walks away thoroughly dejected. This is something he cannot do.

This has *nothing* to do with social balance because Jesus was asking the man to give up *everything*. Jesus knew that the man's faith was in what he owned and in order to be free enough to place his faith in Jesus, he would have to get rid of everything else that vied for his faith. Giving up wealth is not a prerequisite for salvation. However, for the rich, young ruler, his love for and faith in his riches would forever be the one stumbling block that would not allow him to ever see Jesus as the true source of salvation. Jesus told the man to get rid of it for that reason.

As far as the belief that Jesus never judged anyone, anyone's lifestyle, or anyone's beliefs, that is simply not true at all. We see this in a variety of contexts throughout the four gospels.

In one example – John 8 – a woman is caught in adultery. A group of men are ready to stone her but before they do, they want to know what Jesus has to say about it. Should she be stoned as Moses said she should?

Jesus answers the question by telling the men that whichever one of them was without sin could throw the first stone. This normally meant here that only those men who had never been caught in the same sin as the woman were free to carry out the death sentence. Some commentators believe that Jesus was speaking of sinless perfection, which really is not in keeping with everything else He taught on the subject of sin.

Eventually, all the men leave with only the woman remaining. Jesus asks whether there was no one to condemn her and she says they had all left. Jesus affirms He would not condemn her either. But that's not the end of the narrative.

Please note that Jesus ends His conversation with the woman by making a very clear point to her. *"Go. From now on sin no more"* (John 8:11b).

So, did Jesus avoid judging people? Did He refrain from making statements about their lifestyles? No, not at all.

In John 5, we read of the encounter Jesus had with the man at the Pool of Bethesda. Jesus healed the man and afterwards pointedly told him, *"Behold, you have become well; do not sin anymore, so that nothing worse happens to you"* (John 5:14).

In both of these cases, Jesus *forgave* the sins of these individuals. They had sinned and needed forgiving. This is something liberals don't like to deal with because it tends to bring limitations on a person's life – the idea that we need forgiveness for our sins.

In order to forgive a person, a *judgment* has to be made. Jesus obviously judged both people in both cases and found that they needed forgiveness. It is the same with us.

But probably the most misunderstood text of Scripture is the one that quotes Jesus as saying that we should "judge not." That text is found in Matthew 7:1. Jesus is definitely saying that we should not judge. However, the very same Jesus who said not to judge in Matthew 7 also tells us to *"Stop judging by mere appearances, but instead judge correctly"* (John 7:24).

How do we marry these two seeming opposites? It is easy once we understand that in *both* cases, Jesus is essentially saying the same thing. He is telling us not to judge a person's *motives* for doing something. This is why He says that we should stop judging by mere appearances. We think we can see the reason a person does something, but of course, we cannot do that.

When we judge a person's motives, we are judging them based on something we cannot see, but think we can.

This has nothing to do with judging a person's words or actions, something we should do. When Jesus speaks of judging here, He is simply authorizing us to *decide* what is right and wrong, but not the motivation for why someone says or does something.

In other words, Jesus expects us to make a judgment based on moral and theological thinking. We are to discern whether or not all things are good or bad for us to be involved in. Self-righteous, hypocritical, legalistic, unfair and plain wrong judgments are never good or acceptable. Using God-given wisdom and discernment to determine the value of actions or words is what the Christian is to do *daily*. We are *not* to go around vilifying, castigating, or denigrating someone. This is opposed to God and His righteous judgments of us.

Jesus loved *liberally*, but He was avidly strict about fulfilling God's Law as revealed to Moses. Jesus avoided anything that was sin. He judged individuals and their circumstances and offered forgiveness for their sins.

Jesus loved the Father and His will. He dutifully followed the Father's will every day. He was not some politically correct left-leaning liberal of His day. He was certainly not a social liberal. He was, in fact, very traditional when it came to God's Law. He was strict and would not set aside any portion of it, but ensured that He fulfilled all of it.

This is not the lifestyle of a pluralistic liberal. It is the lifestyle of a conservative who fully believed that there was one way and only one way to God, the Father. That way happened to be through Jesus, God the Son (cf. John 14:6).

Chapter 9

Politically Correct Politics

T he more things change, the more they remain the same. We've all heard that saying before and as strange as it may sound, the truth that emerges from it is undeniable. This is especially so within the confines of politics and political history.

Yet many today either do not know or deny the truth about the Democratic Party especially. It is seen as the party that helps the poor and underprivileged. But does it?

"The first thing you need to know about the Democratic Party is that its first vice president, the traitor Aaron Burr, shot and killed one of the Founding Fathers, Alexander Hamilton, and then plotted sedition

against his own president. Everything else is, as they say, commentary."[53]

Walsh continues by stating what many seem not to realize about the Democratic Party: *"IT IS ONE of the ironies of American history that the Democratic Party has managed to pass itself off as the champion of the underdog and the crusader for equal rights. The actual history of the Democratic Party – distinct from the history of some individual Democrats – tells a very different story. It is a history in which the lust for power, not a concern for the poor and dispossessed, looms large. This story is seldom told. Indeed, so successful has been the suppression of the true history of the Democratic Party for the sake of the 'narrative' that simply laying out the facts appears as a startling forensic exercise, a brief."*[54]

When we stop to consider the fact that the Democratic Party has not only been able to change its spots, but many within this party fail to understand or believe the truth about it, we cannot help but wonder. Are people really that thick when it comes to discerning the truth regarding the Democratic Party, or do they simply believe "that was then; this is now"? In either case, it seems that for many people, the Democratic Party is the party that exists to fight for the downtrodden and hindered.

Yet look at what the Democratic Party does to even black individuals who deign to be conservative in mindset. For a long time now, Allen West (who lost his re-election bid in a very questionable election in Florida) has been labeled an "Uncle Tom" as well as other things by those from the Democratic Party. *"The phrase 'Uncle Tom' has also become an epithet for a person who is slavish and excessively subservient to perceived authority figures, particularly a black person who be-*

---

[53] Walsh, Michael (2012-07-17). The People v. the Democratic Party (Kindle Locations 34-36). Perseus Books Group. Kindle Edition.
[54] Walsh, Michael (2012-07-17). The People v. the Democratic Party (Kindle Locations 19-24). Perseus Books Group. Kindle Edition.

haves in a subservient manner to <u>white people</u>; *or any person perceived to be a participant in the oppression of their own group. The negative epithet is the result of later works derived from the original novel*"[55] (emphasis in original).

So, any black person who is conservative is roundly rejected as someone who caters to white people, thus the label "Uncle Tom." This label tends to redefine the individual as duplicitous; therefore, their words should be rejected.

This is what the politically correct do because they are not at all interested in having an honest discussion. They are only interested in rebuking and ultimately silencing. Because of his views, Dr. Ben Carson joined the ranks of "Uncle Toms" in America, labeled that way by other blacks and/or Democrats within the politically correct arena.

Carson joins not only Allen West, but Colin Powell, Condoleeza Rice, U. S. Supreme Court Justice Clarence Thomas (referred to as "Uncle Tom Justice" by Time magazine), Herman Cain, and others. The obvious conclusion is that any black who is a conservative is seen as supporting white people while turning his/her back on blacks. The belief propagated by the Democrats is that blacks are treated as real people when they align themselves with the causes and policies of Democrats.

Michael Walsh argues that since the "*inception of the Republic, the Democratic Party has been a public enemy – an organization antithetical to our nation's traditions, civic virtues, and moral values.*"[56] That may seem like a huge overstatement, but if one considers the policies and laws that the Democratic Party has pursued, it certainly cannot be considered far-fetched.

---

[55] http://shark-tank.net/2013/04/01/ben-carson-joins-allen-wests-elite-uncle-tom-fraternity/ (04/02/2013)

[56] Walsh, Michael (2012-07-17). The People v. the Democratic Party (Kindle Locations 41-42). Perseus Books Group. Kindle Edition.

Then again, Walsh notes, "*Consider the facts. Whether it has been defending slavery, selling out our secrets, or simply voting 'present' so as not to take a stand on the crucial moral issues of both statecraft and soul-craft, the party of slavery, segregation, secularism, and sedition has always been in the forefront of everything inimical to the United States of America.*"[57]

But what is even more interesting is how the thinking of the Democratic Party became part and parcel of much of the GOP as well. Walsh says this occurred because in the late 60s, many Democrats jumped over to the GOP without adopting the policies and tenets of faith of the Republican Party.

The net result of this is that the racists who were deeply embedded in the Democratic Party were now part of the GOP. Walsh states, "*modern Democrats have adopted as an article of faith the bedtime story that, thanks to Tricky Dick Nixon's 'southern strategy,' the racists who had been the backbone of their party for the better part of a century suddenly switched to the GOP en masse some time around 1968, with the happy result that now all the racists are on the right. Presto — instant virtuousness and a clean slate!*"[58]

Is it any wonder that within the GOP, we have people like Chris Christie, John McCain, Lindsay Graham, and too many others to mention who superficially appear to be Republicans, but when it comes to their voting, too often side with those on the left? This is due to the fact that though they like to say they are "moderates," in truth, they are much further to the left than they would like anyone to believe.

Many of these individuals pontificate, pound the pulpit, and even criticize the Obama administration, yet when push comes to shove, they

---

[57] Walsh, Michael (2012-07-17). The People v. the Democratic Party (Kindle Locations 44-47). Perseus Books Group. Kindle Edition.
[58] http://pjmedia.com/michaelwalsh/2013/03/28/history-lesson/?singlepage=true (04/02/2013)

are too often found *supporting* this very same administration that they are heard condemning. Something is out of whack and it has to do with the fact that decades ago, Democrats either jumped ship to become part of the GOP (while retaining their own liberal mindset) or they came to realize that though they were inwardly Democrats, running as a GOP was a way to gain the office. This also allowed them to pretend to be conservative while doing what they could to vote for liberal policies while on the "right."

Ultimately, at this point in time, it does not really matter if a person is a Republican or a Democrat. It matters how they *vote,* and as Walsh points out, too many of these individuals simply vote "present" in order to avoid being judged by their vote later on.

With the most recent presidential election of November 2012, I saw just how corrupt things are in politics. To me, it seems as though that event confirmed just how controlled both parties are and in fact, the entire voting process seems to have been wrested from the hands of the voters. Nothing is being left up to chance now because the politically correct left has things it needs to accomplish.

What is interesting (but certainly not surprising) is that Obama has created an elections commission through another one of his executive orders. Supposedly, it is *"designed to find ways to make voting easier."*[59] That is really odd considering how hard Obama worked to keep our own military from voting via absentee ballot.[60] The left spun this to their advantage while stating that the right is lying about the whole thing. In truth, Obama did not believe that the military should be afforded *extra* time to vote. Yet why does something tell me that if he knew ahead of time that the majority of military people

---

[59] http://www.usatoday.com/story/news/politics/2013/03/28/obama-election-commission-bauer-ginsberg/2028547/ (04/02/2013)
[60] http://blog.heritage.org/2012/08/06/keeping-the-military-from-voting-in-ohio/ (04/02/2013)

would have been in *support* of him, his administration would never have taken up the issue in the first place?

Then again, the left has always tried to outrun its own bad press. If they can't outrun it, they'll simply change sides (as Walsh notes many did in 1968). In another article, we learn that *"It makes [Democrats] profoundly uncomfortable that among the 21 who voted **against** the Civil Rights Act of 1964 can be found Albert Arnold Gore, Sr., the founder of the Hillbilly Dynasty; Robert "KKK" Byrd, the Conscience of the Senate; and Sleepin' Sam Ervin of Watergate fame"*[61] (emphasis added).

Democrats do not like to own up to their onerous history. The truth is there, but they will do anything to sweep it away or reimagine it. Inherent in their political policies are things that seem to *favor* blacks and other persons of color and one has to wonder why this is the case.

The answer is bound up within the confines of racism. *"Democrats who argue that the best policies for black Americans are those that are soft on crime and generous with welfare are engaged in much the same sort of cynical racial calculation President Johnson was practicing when he informed skeptical southern governors that his plan for the Great Society was 'to have them niggers voting Democratic for the next two hundred years.' Johnson's crude racism is, happily, largely a relic of the past, but his strategy endures."*[62]

In fact, Johnson's racism still exists, in the opinion of this author. It is simply couched in verbiage and actions that *appear* to care for minorities, especially blacks. The end result is that the Democrats gain allegiance from individuals who gain from entitlements. It is the proverbial "you scratch my back and I'll scratch yours" mentality. Of

---

[61] http://pjmedia.com/michaelwalsh/2013/03/28/history-lesson/?singlepage=true (04/02/2013)
[62] Ibid

course, it is understood that the blacks who benefit from entitlements are none the wiser for it.

Ultimately, whether catering to poor blacks or illegal aliens via entitlements and giveaways, Democrats *have* to cater to minorities because it is the only way they can be guaranteed any voters at all. The more of these types of voters they create, the better their chances of winning will be in the future.

Chapter 10

Politically Correct Infanticide

In what has got to be the most ridiculous as well as anti-human rhetoric heard yet, a lobbyist for Planned Parenthood was quoted as saying that a post-abortive baby who survives the procedure should *not* automatically be given medical aid. This was stated before a Florida legislature that was considering a bill to force medical practitioners to provide medical care to in these types of situations.

When asked what she meant by her comments, the woman, "*Alisa LaPolt Snow, the lobbyist representing the Florida Alliance of Planned Parenthood Affiliates, testified that her organization believes **the decision to kill an infant who survives a failed abortion should be left***

up to the woman seeking an abortion and her abortion doctor"[63] (emphasis in original).

Essentially, what LaPolt Snow was advocating is a *post-birth abortion*. So, in the case where a child who is being aborted (deliberately murdered) survives the process, Planned Parenthood wants everyone to know that whether or not the baby is given life-saving medical procedures is between the woman and the doctor.

Obviously, for a child to survive and live after an attempted abortion, that child would have to be well along in development. We are not talking about a child that is a few weeks or a month along. We are talking about a child that is very close to natural birth in order for it to be able to survive outside the womb like this.

Even though this would be the case – with a baby surviving an attempted abortion – Planned Parenthood will still refuse to discuss the child as a human being at this point. Planned Parenthood says that the child can still be *killed*, if that's what the mother wants to happen.

This is not really abortion, *per se*. It is full on *eugenics*. It is the determined effort to eliminate people from society through infanticide: murder of newly born human beings that is condoned by the state under the guise of "women's rights."

Yet, in spite of the ramifications of this atrocity, Planned Parenthood released a statement that confirms their support for the lobbyist who made the statements. Their statement reads as follows:

> *Last week, a panel of Florida state legislators demanded speculation about a vague set of extremely unlikely and highly unusual medical circumstances. Medical guidelines and ethics already compel physicians facing life-*

> *threatening circumstances to respond, and Planned*
> *Parenthood physicians provide high-quality medical care*
> *and adhere to the most rigorous professional standards,*
> *including providing emergency care. In the extremely un-*
> *likely event that the scenario presented by the panel of*
> *legislators should happen, of course Planned Parenthood*
> *would provide appropriate care to both the woman and*
> *the infant.*[64]

The tragedy in the above statement has to do with the amount of lies inherent within it. They call this situation a "highly unusual medical" situation. Planned Parenthood wants us to believe this would never happen, but according to an undercover video from 2009, it *has* happened. Even if it happens *once*, the law-makers wanted to pass a law that would force medical personnel to do what they could to save a life.

But also notice that the statement really says nothing. It does not state unequivocally that Planned Parenthood doctors would do everything they could to save the child's life. The statement simply states that they would *"provide appropriate care,"* which means nothing and can be taken several ways.

The sad truth is that babies born alive – surviving an abortion attempt – happens too often.[65] This seems to be a norm within the underbelly of abortions that occurs every day in America. Women are told to simply "void" their child (through childbirth) into a toilet, and examples of this "appropriate care" by Planned Parenthood can be clearly seen of Abortionist James Pendergraft IV, who went on trial in 2011 for injuries sustained by a pre-born baby during an abortion.

---

[64] http://www.lifenews.com/2013/04/02/new-planned-parenthood-statement-defends-pro-infanticide-remarks/ (04/02/2013)
[65] http://www.lifenews.com/2011/07/27/babies-born-alive-in-toilets-at-abortion-center-left-to-die/ (04/02/2013)

He ultimately was found liable and ordered to pay $36,737,660.16 to the plaintiff.[66]

Infanticide is quickly becoming a new normal in late-term abortion clinics, where children are born alive. Even though they cannot survive by themselves, they are either left unattended to die or caused to die by cutting the spinal cord at the neck.

The saddest part of this whole thing is that too many women have repeat abortions. They do it because it's easier than having and raising a child.

Planned Parenthood is in the business of abortions to make money. If there was no money in it, they wouldn't be doing it. Though Planned Parenthood likes to tout the alleged fact that they provide quality healthcare, the truth is that their mainstay is in killing unborn children because there is a huge profit in it. Much of their money comes from federal dollars, which means that every person who pays taxes helps to pay for the murder of unborn children and, in a growing number of cases, the murder of post-abortive babies through infanticide.

Just recently, the Obama administration once again provided more money to Planned Parenthood to the tune of a $2.3 million dollar grant.[67] That should keep them going for a while! The money goes toward Planned Parenthood's "Teens Rise!" program, designed to help students understand the difference between "continuous abstinence" and "celibate abstinence."

Of course, the information would not be complete without a connection to another portion of the website that *provides a link to the*

---

[66] http://www.lifenews.com/2011/07/27/babies-born-alive-in-toilets-at-abortion-center-left-to-die/ (04/02/2013)

[67] http://www.lifenews.com/2013/04/01/obama-admin-gives-2-3m-grant-to-planned-parenthood-abortion-biz/ (04/02/2013)

'ABC's' page where graphic descriptions of sexual acts and condom and other contraceptive uses are posted."[68]

Then again, those who align themselves with Planned Parenthood seem to go out of their way to denigrate the value of a preborn child, referring the child as a "thing" or misdirecting the conversation by once again placing the blame on men; according to one commentator at MSNBC, all religions were created by men, so it's obvious (to her) that men simply want to control women.[69]

This is an oft-repeated claim within politically correct circles. It is the left's effort to highlight men as "aggressors" who want to keep women (in this case) victimized through a form of slavery. The "slavery" here is the repression of "healthcare" rights for women by trying to reverse the decision that made abortion legal. So, conservative men are painted as the true "oppressors" of women and their rights. This plays well in the media, and of course, men who are on the left can play along by echoing this sentiment on their own shows.

Few consider how asinine this line of reasoning it is, but it works and works well because it taps into the emotions of women especially. If someone can become righteously upset over the idea that men want to keep women "barefoot and pregnant," that is seen as reason enough to believe that the lie being promulgated by the politically correct left is *truth*, in spite of the fact that it is not truth.

The same female commentator who speaks of men wanting to be in charge of women wonders, *"why isn't religion as concerned about water and economic justice and all these things as it is and as they mentioned sexual morality"*?[70]

---

[68] http://www.lifenews.com/2013/04/01/obama-admin-gives-2-3m-grant-to-planned-parenthood-abortion-biz/ (04/02/2013)
[69] http://www.lifenews.com/2013/04/02/once-again-msnbc-talking-head-calls-unborn-babies-things/ (04/02/2013)
[70] Ibid

This, of course, is a not-so-subtle way of implying that religion is only concerned about repressing women; therefore, we see its hypocrisy. It isn't true, but again, that does not matter. The question asked *seems* to have an air of truth about it; therefore, to many people, it *is* true.

Political correctness works through society, endeavoring to replace absolute truth with a paltry substitute. It continues because there are too many individuals who do not seem to grasp the fact that truth is not determined by how a person feels about it. Truth is truth and there can only be one truth for all people, not a truth for this group and another truth for that group.

Sadly, infanticide is becoming a recognized truth for too many people. It is the deliberate murder of post-abortive babies. Christians need to stand against this abomination, even if we never successfully get the practice outlawed. We need to let the world know where we stand, whether they are ever willing to see any merit in our position or not.

People who call themselves Christian while believing that abortion itself is okay, or that infanticide – though sad – is better off for the child, completely miss the point. God said "thou shalt not kill," which as we know means that premeditated murder has no place in a society that claims to be civilized.

Abortion is nothing more than premeditated murder. It is the deliberate killing of an unborn (or sometimes *post-abortive*) child and it is wrong. What I find fascinating is that those who claim to be Christian will normally respond with a reference to some military action or war as being just as reprehensible as abortion. The two do not equate, except in their minds. Certainly, God never equated the two.

Regardless of whether or not abortion is ever outlawed (and it's doubtful that it will be), we need to stand with God on this issue. He has specifically stated that murder is not an option. This applies to desiring to kill someone out of jealousy or hatred (or for hire). It also applies to the killing of the unborn child because as far as God is concerned, life begins at conception.

It is not up to us to apply our emotional virtue to a situation God has already ruled on. He said it and He speaks the truth because He is the truth. We cannot overrule God and avoid the consequences of that action. We will reap what we sow and unfortunately, it is very clear that society throughout America is reaping what it has been sowing for decades. The chickens are coming home to roost and we do not know how much longer God's patience will extend to us.

I cannot imagine that it will be that much longer.

================== Chapter 11 ==================
Politically Correct "Uncle Toms"

For anyone who has not been paying attention, Dr. Ben Carson has come under severe fire from the left for his conservative views. Carson, as many know, gave a speech at the National Prayer breakfast (which was attended by the Obamas) and he was roundly panned as someone who was disrespectful in Obama's presence because of the things he said and/or implied.

What is truly amazing is that Carson – like Allen West, Sen. Ted Cruz, and other conservative blacks or persons of color – is *himself* black, and yet, when those on the left (both white *and* black) disagree with Carson, they have no problem calling him out. They seem to enjoy verbally castigating him because he is not only conservative, but *black* as well. Apparently, there is an unwritten law that frowns upon minorities having conservative values. It's called *political correctness*.

On a recent episode of the Mark Levin radio show, Levin pointed out that it seems as though these liberal racists (many of them white) do what they do because Carson has dared to come off the "plantation" and speak his mind about the problems in America that have nothing to do with the policies of conservatism, but of political ness.[71] Carson notes that it is political correctness that is destroying this country because those within the politically correct camp are doing everything they possibly can to shut down discourse with which they disagree. They want no one else to be heard. It is their opinion or shut up. Carson refers to these people as *white racist detractors* whose verbal assault on him he describes as "vicious."[72]

It amazes me to realize that if anyone who happens to be a person of color steps up to offer his or her conservative perspective, the whole thing is simply labeled another attempt of the GOP to cover their own alleged racism by using a person of color for their own ends. This, in and of itself, is a racist sentiment, but since the Democrats and the left pride themselves on allegedly being free of racism, it obviously stands that their comments cannot be racist, but are *true*. It is clear that too many people in America are not aware of the accurate history of the Democrat Party in the United States.

The Daily Kos states, "*The NY Times' flattering profile of the very professionally accomplished Dr. Ben Carson is part of a concerted effort to make a compelling news story out of the Republican Party's search for a viable black presidential candidate.*

---

[71] http://legalinsurrection.com/2013/04/white-liberals-dont-like-being-called-racist/ (04/03/2013)
[72] Ibid

"The Republican Party's quest is more of a comedic tragedy than a drama. It is a rerun of bad serialized television. Carson today; Herman Cain yesterday; Allen West before then; Colin Powell years ago. The story always ends the same way, with the masters of the Tea Party GOP going onto the next one in search of a black political messiah who can successfully package and sell a set of policies that are hostile to people of color, and which no black or brown folks with any self-respect or common sense, would support."[73]

Of course, the Daily Kos has no problem in the same article referring to Carson as the GOP's newest "Mandingo," which in and of itself seems racist. They would simply argue, though, that they are merely pointing out the "truth" of the Republican Party.

Aside from this, where do they get the idea that the GOP is behind Carson's rise? He's been writing books for a number of years as well as having been invited numerous places as keynote speaker. The fact that he is on this show or that one does not prove that the GOP is behind it. It simply proves that Carson is another conservative the left loves to hate. Could that be why he's in demand?

With one fell swoop, those at the Daily Kos state that no person of color would have anything to do with conservative values that founded this country. That's an assumption on their part that is wholly without merit, but like most within the politically correct arena, they will say it anyway, regardless of its truthfulness.

That's what political correctness tells us, but is it true? Not according to many blacks and other persons of color who obviously *can* think for themselves and have chosen conservatism over political correctness. These folks see what the *real* racists like Al Sharpton, Jesse

---

[73] http://www.dailykos.com/story/2013/03/26/1197163/–Introducing-Ben-Carson-the-Newest-Black-Conservative-Political-Mandingo-for-The-Tea-Party-GOP (04/03/2013)

Jackson, Maxine Waters, and all the rest are doing to continue the racist lies that have helped instigate racism in society.

Rev. Jesse Lee Peterson, founder of BOND Action (Brotherhood Organization of a New Destiny) states in a recent newsletter, *"Tension is mounting daily among the races. Black leaders push the lie that white Americans are the cause of black problems, not the lack of fathers in black homes. Growing violence toward whites – coming from young black men – is eroding our cities. Almost no one will speak out – not the President, Attorney General, mayors, police chiefs, or parents. White Americans are bewildered. Most want peace among the races. But they have no idea how to accomplish it...Most black Americans today are suffering not from racism but the lack of moral character. White Americans have a moral obligation to be honest with them – not appease them!"*[74]

In one of his books, *SCAM*, Peterson highlights the troubling problem of *"how the black leadership exploits black America."* Peterson takes the time to underscore several important points that are consistently missed by both black leaders and white liberals. He repudiates the likes of Jesse Jackson, notes that Farrakhan is America's answer to Hitler, and points out that Al Sharpton seems to be the "riot king" of America.

Rev. Peterson – a black man himself – is out to educate blacks *and* whites, as well as to do what he can to mend fences between races. He wants white people to know that we should not fear and our "cowardice" actually does more to hurt the black person than help him.

"The threat of being labeled 'racist' causes whites to cower to the wishes of blacks and hold their tongues when they see things amiss in the

---

[74] BOND September 1, 2012, p. 1

black community. The fact is that the civil rights 'leaders' and elite liberal Democrats are much at fault for the poor condition of the black community, not so-called white racists.

"But, having largely given in to their lies, white culture is suffering, not only because blacks are free to be immoral without complaint but also because many whites now lack character as a result of giving in to this fear for so long.

"As whites allowed themselves to be paralyzed from fear, legitimate black leaders were pushed aside by racial scam artists. These phony leaders then consolidated power over blacks, and the result has been an ever-increasing level of immorality within the black community.

"Compounding the problem, the sins of the parents are passed down through the generations. As a result of whites not standing up in the past, this same weakness and lack of character is repeated in the new generation. The idea of being called 'racist' is as horrific to them as ever, and whites of the new generation have been silenced because of their parents' poor example."[75]

This induced fear (of being called "racist") is what white liberals and black race-baiters create. In fact, this is what the politically correct left does *best* with their incendiary labeling. Whether they call someone a hater, a sexist, bigot, or racist, the intent is the same. It is to shut the person down, to shame them into silence, because ultimately, the left is not interested in discussion or dialogue. They are interested only in putting forth their opinion and shutting off all who disagree with it. There is something terribly dangerous about this mentality that is certainly growing within America.

---

[75] Rev. Jesse Lee Peterson, SCAM (2003), pp. 85-86

Peterson himself acknowledges this problem. *"Taking a stand for what is right has put me at odds with the civil rights establishment. I have endured all kinds of name-calling and intimidation tactics. I have personally been called 'n*gger,' 'sellout,' 'Uncle Tom,' and many other names. But I understand that I am fighting against evil. These names mean nothing to me. They are the pitiful words of cowards who do not have right on their side. By letting them pass, I am able to continue standing up for what is right: the emancipation of black America and the disbandment of the current black leadership. It is now time for white Americans to realize that they are part of this same battle. Enduring these attacks is part of a blessed life. I know that whenever a person stands up for right he will be subject to such attacks."*[76]

Dr. Ben Carson is now in the spotlight and is the newest target of the racists on the left. They will continue to spew their hateful rhetoric at him, insisting that he is only getting his 15 minutes of fame because the GOP is looking for "new minority blood" or "messiah."

The fact that Carson is a strong supporter of the conservative *and* biblical values inherent within this country is something that they cannot focus on because of their politically correct stance. They have to lay the blame on some systemic racism that is allegedly built into those on the right side of the aisle. This is in spite of larger-than-life Democrats who wielded their racism like clubs to keep blacks "in their place." The Democrats haven't really changed their spots. They have simply changed the way they *appear* to people. The message has changed, but not the intent, which is to keep blacks and other minorities chained to the government's entitlement programs.

People like Allen West, Ben Carson, Rev. Peterson and others are dutifully ignored or panned by the politically correct left. They cannot allow the opinion of these conservatives to stand without attacking

---

[76] Rev. Jesse Lee Peterson, SCAM (2003), pp. 87

them. It's a sad state when people must reduce themselves to the lowered position of instigating hatred toward someone because they hold an opposite opinion.

The idea that Ben Carson (or any other person of color) is not smart enough to arrive to his own conclusions by himself but must have gotten there as a puppet used by the GOP is not only ridiculous, but self-serving to the politically correct leftists that cry and scream about people like him. Carson is an educated man and understands the true history of this nation (unlike most who stage their diversionary tactics from the left side of the aisle).

In one video response to Carson, Bob Beckel states that Dr. Carson *infuriates* him because of his position and because he lumps all liberals together. Beckel is *always* lumping conservatives together, but apparently, that's fine. He also opens his remarks by stating that Dr. Carson is not important. Really, Bob? Then why even discuss him?

Beckel points out that he and many other liberals marched with other civil rights activists in the 1960s for equality. So did conservatives, but the other truth is that the liberals of *today* are *not* the same as liberals of the 1960s. The mindset is completely different between the two groups. There is no connection between the leftists of today and the leftists of five decades ago. Attitudes have changed way too much since the 1960s.

In their efforts to classify the GOP or conservatives in general as racists, politically correct leftists make the foolhardy assumption that the *truth* of their own actions (and words) will not be realized. Yet their racism *is* seen and understood. Their desire to stifle conversation knows no bounds. It is very clear that what they are underneath all of their huffing, puffing, and labeling is the very epitome of what they accuse others of being.

Chapter 12
Politically Correct Violence

People like Rev. Jesse Lee Peterson, Colin Flaherty, Taleeb Starkes, and others have noticed and warned us about an uptick in black on white violence that goes relatively unnoticed by the media. This appears to be the case because of the politically correct motivation *of* the media and those in power, like police chiefs, mayors, and others.

The sad truth is that while this growing violence occurs, innocent whites are often the victims of that violence toward them solely because they are white and for no other reason. Tragically, too many in the black (and white) community look the other way, pretending it doesn't exist. I've read all sorts of reasons why it's not reported, everything from saving the black community from embarrassment to not wanting to stoke fears among whites. Whatever the reason, the truth seems to be that it *needs* to be reported *and* dealt with because people are breaking the law. It will not stop by itself.

Recently, blogger Jeffrey Carter related to us that on one particular Saturday, roughly 500 or so young people stormed into the Michigan Avenue shopping area of Chicago. He states that most of the young people were black.[77] Carter relates how these young people organized via their social networks, choosing where to go and when, along with what they would do when they got there.

Another article on a separate website highlights the same incident. There, we learn that *"several teens were arrested after dozens of mob groups began attacking pedestrians on Chicago's downtown Magnificent Mile area on Saturday night. Police responded to reports of disturbances near Michigan and Chicago Avenues. Police said 28 teens were arrested during the incident and no serious injuries were reported."*[78]

Interestingly enough, the article never refers to the ethnicity of any of the perpetrators or the victims. Some would say if they did it would be unnecessarily incendiary. Those, like me, who believe it is important (just as important as when a "white-Hispanic" shoots a young black male) are likely to be called bigots or racists for wanting to know. But there is a good reason for wanting to know. Does this type of incident tell us that anger is building up in the black community toward whites? Is all of this just random or is it predicated on the assumption that blacks can attack whites and get away with it?

---

[77] http://pointsandfigures.com/2013/04/01/the-new-chicago-mob/ (04/04/2013)
[78] http://usnews.nbcnews.com/_news/2013/04/01/17547970-hundreds-of-teens-mob-pedestrians-on-chicagos-magnificent-mile?lite (04/04/2013)

Author Colin Flaherty provides a good deal of insight in his book *White Girl Bleed a Lot*. His byline – *the return of racial violence to America* – tells us (if true) that something has gone wrong and needs fixing in America.

The reality seems to be that what has gone wrong has been created by the political correctness that has infiltrated society. If whites are seen as the essential "aggressor" (as political correctness teaches), it stands to reason that minorities are viewed as the "victim." In this case, the implication is that minorities have to "fight" to be free of the "aggressor."

Slavery *is* part of the tragic underbelly of America's past, and though for most of us, it *is* behind us, it is clear that there are many (and a growing number of blacks) who are doing their best to bring it to and keep it in the present. This allows them to be "angry" almost all the time at white people and they are excused for their anger.

Certainly, there are some blacks alive today who dealt with the terrible racism that was on display by many of our nation's politicians in the 1960s. They stood with Dr. Martin Luther King, Jr. and marched with him to improve efforts of blacks not only in the south, but in all parts of America.

Yet when I read books about or by King or watch speeches he offered, I do not see the same type of seething anger that many blacks seem to traffic in today. For many of them, it seems like the issue of slavery – which did *not* directly affect them years ago (because they were not alive then) – is merely a useful tool that they can grab hold of and wield against any and all whites.

This is *not* to say or imply that racism is gone! It is *not* gone. It is still here and as we have already discovered, much of it comes from liberal whites who seem to want to keep blacks chained to the government's entitle teat. The idea that these blacks could emancipate themselves from the government's programs does not bode well with the left because these same blacks would then not feel beholden to the left and might even vote for a conservative candidate. Oh, the *horrors*!

Isn't this what Dr. Ben Carson was referring to when we discussed his situation a few chapters back? The truth is that white liberals are some of the worst racists going, but they do everything they can to *hide* their racist views from their constituency. They are desperate to keep blacks on the plantation (as Carson states) because they can continue to control them.

Are their leaders really helping them? It certainly does not appear to be the case. Since the Rodney King verdict aftermath, has the situation improved for people of color in Los Angeles? Why not? Why aren't people like Maxine Waters doing anything better for the people of her district?

Every time there's a problem, someone like Al Sharpton is sure to swoop in, get his face on TV, make threatening gestures, and do whatever it takes to make blacks look like the victims. Unfortunately, this simply confirms to these folks that this is the way the game is played. They must continue to be seen as victims, so that society and government will continue to offer handouts.

When they break the law, they will be given slaps on the wrist. Of course, this does not apply to all black people or other people of color, but it appears to be a growing trend that is occurring throughout society today. It is tragic because black people are continually treated by white liberal racists as though they are stupid and cannot really handle life, so they must be guided through life by white elitists on the left who portray themselves as truly caring for blacks and minorities. Yet, their actual situations never improve! They continue to live in the same hovels and run-down communities. They are always given something, which not only takes away their self-respect but mires them in the continued problem of never being able to climb out of their pit.

How many presidents – including Obama – have we heard talk about rebuilding the infrastructure? Well? Why isn't it being done in low-income communities where many of these people want desperately to see themselves as self-supporting people who have something to be proud of in their lives?

Instead, the government simply continues to hand out EBT and SNAP debit cards and "takes care" of them as if they are children. I'm not saying we need to get rid of welfare. I'm simply saying that at some point, people need to learn to be self-sufficient, and the government is doing *nothing* to make that happen.

So, the black young people who are coming up in this current generation have learned that the government will continue to care for them. They also learn that the same government will often look the other way when they "act out." It's kind of like being a member of a rich family that gets to slide when they break the law because their money covers a multitude of their sins.

This is what is happening in too many black communities. But it's certainly not just black communities. Communities that are made up of other minorities are also given a pass. Illegal aliens are allowed to gather en masse in protesting the immigration policies of the United States. They are allowed to disrespect the flag of our nation and when someone steps in to stop it, *they* are arrested.

Colin Flaherty's book highlights the problem of growing agitation toward whites because whites are the "aggressor" and all minorities are "victims" doing what they can to get out from under the oppression of whites. What these minorities fail to realize, of course, is that the people who make the decisions are, for the most part, still white, but since it appears to them that they are in their corner, they never make the connection that these white liberals could possibly be racist.

Flaherty highlights the fact that "*since 2010, groups of black people are roaming the streets of America – assaulting, intimidating, stalking, threatening, vandalizing, stealing, shooting, stabbing, even raping and killing.*"[79] This is obviously not good. Something is happening that needs attention, yet Flaherty also notes that no one is even noticing it. They are all too busy ignoring it.

"*But local media and public officials are silent. Crime is color blind, says a Milwaukee police chief. Race is not important, a Chicago newspaper editor assures us.*

"*That denies the obvious: America is the most race conscious society in the world.*

"*We learn that every day from the black caucuses, black teachers, black unions, black ministers, black colleges, black high schools, black music, black moguls, black hair business owners, black public employees, black art, black names, black poets, black inventors, black soldiers, black police officers.*

"*We learn it from the National Association of Black Journalists.*

"*We talk about everything except black mob violence and lawlessness. That is Taboo.*"[80]

---

[79] Colin Flaherty *White Girl Bleed a Lot* (2012), p. 14
[80] Ibid, p. 14

Flaherty goes on to list nearly 40 major cities where black on white violence has become a sort of norm. In one particular case, on the Fourth of July in Milwaukee, "*after looting a nearby convenience store, a crowd of nearly 100 blacks set upon some white teens on a picnic. After one white women, a black woman noted 'Oh, white girl bleed a lot'.*"[81]

The tragedy is that, according to Flaherty, these types of incidents are not uncommon. In fact, they are becoming far more common. Not only that, but what is often reported in the media barely resembles the actual event itself.

A year or so ago, there were any number of these types of events occurring at fairs throughout the country in which gangs of blacks would gather together for the express purpose of beating up on whites. The numbers were almost always minimized and rarely, if ever, were the perpetrators' (or victims') ethnicities mentioned.

These facts only came out after people who actually witnessed the events (and took photos, video, or both) posted their information on the 'Net. It became quite clear that something very troubling was happening and both public officials and the media were remiss in reporting the truth of the events.

As an example, Flaherty notes that in Wilmington, Delaware, one lone bicyclist was surrounded by "*a mob of 20 black people*"[82]. They knocked him down and took his bicycle. As far as the newspaper was concerned, "*only four people actually put their hands on the cyclist. So the newspaper said only four people were involved. This kind of math happens a lot.*"[83]

---

[81] Colin Flaherty *White Girl Bleed a Lot* (2012), p. 16
[82] Ibid, p. 16
[83] Ibid, p. 16

So in this case, we see that the newspaper article lied by omission. Yet, in other instances, people lie by commission. *"In Chicago, after weeks of racial violence where the newspapers refused to mention the crime was almost exclusively black gangs on individual whites, the Superintendent of the Police said he knew what was causing the violence: Sarah Palin."*[84] The absurdity of this is self-evident. Then again, we are talking about Garry F. McCarthy, that Rahm Emanuel appointed as Police Superintendent. McCarthy is not known for his common sense.

Many of these ugly events of black on white crime would not be known except for the fact that the victims came forward with their stories and, in many cases, video or photos of the incidents. In too many cases, police refused to arrest anyone or even make inquiries.

Flaherty also notes that many victims prefer not to discuss the race of their attackers because they believe that in some way, it is either divisive or racist altogether. People should just be people, right?

It would appear that many whites have bought the lie that says they must be color blind, even when their attackers are not. This is part of the "white privilege" argument that is supposed to instill white guilt within white people throughout society.

It is supposed to cause white people to feel ashamed of what they have "done" to blacks, to hold their head in disgrace, and to actually come to believe that they deserve the treatment they are receiving at the hands of racist blacks. This mentality is wrong, but there aren't too many black leaders who are standing against it. In their own way, they are encouraging it among young blacks today.

---

[84] Colin Flaherty *White Girl Bleed a Lot* (2012), p. 17

Chapter 13
Still MORE Politically Correct Violence!

Years ago, I lived in Philadelphia for a few years while attending what was then Philadelphia College of Bible. The year I graduated – 1979 – was the last year the college remained in Center City on Arch Street. It relocated shortly after graduation from just outside Philly to Langhorne Manor, PA.

I recall those days in Philly as being relatively safe. In fact, I never came to harm while living there, even when I went out at night. This is not to say that things did not happen, of course. It was (and remains) a large city and crime happened.

However, I am learning just how dangerous this same city has become. The City of Brotherly Love is becoming well-known for its racial crime and much of it appears to be black on white crime. In fact, one group – *Council of Conservative Citizens* – has issued a major alert due to racially motivated hate crimes occurring there.[85]

The council's alert states:

> *Over the last two years the city of Philadelphia, Pennsylvania has been a nationwide trend-setter in violent hate and bias motivated crimes targeting whites committed by blacks.*

> *The Council of Conservative Citizens has compiled data from reported crimes in and around the city of Philadelphia that clearly demonstrate a trend in which the white population in the region is being targeted by the blacks in the city for acts of violence based solely on their race.*

> *An extremely high threat of violence against white people in the city of Philadelphia has been identified by the Council of Conservative Citizens. It is recommended that white people avoid the city as much as possible, especially the City Center area around Market and Chestnut.[86]*

The City Center area is right where I used to live and walk. In fact, I recall jogging up to the Art Museum past Logan's Circle often. It appears, based on a number of reports (and not just those from the Council of Conservative Citizens either), that Philadelphia has taken on a new attitude where race matters and whites are in season. Apparently, the threat is real enough to prompt another group – *Una-*

---

[85] http://cofcc.org/2012/02/cofcc-issues-major-alert-over-hate-crimes-in-philadelphia/ (04/05/2013)
[86] Ibid

musement Park – to produce a flyer in the hopes that people will take precautions.

Council of Conservative Citizens (which some have accused of being a racist organization) has even gone so far as to put together a map identifying areas where 23 racially motivated crimes occurred over a 26 month period.[87]

If you'll take the time to click on the individual crimes listed on the left of the page that comes up (from the link below), you will learn more about each crime.

You might also note that many of these crimes occurred during the day. The mobs of black youths were small to large while picking out one or two whites at a time.

The current tragedy is complicated by the fact that in many cases, white victims are often ignored, as if what they went through is no big deal. *"The Southern Poverty Law Center (SPLC), claims to 'track' and 'fight' hate crimes. However the list of hate crimes on their website are usually minor acts of vandalism, graffiti, and things that happened a long time ago. Robert Steinback of the SPLC insulted the White victims of Philadelphia hate crimes by saying it was just a 'coincident fac-*

---

[87] https://maps.google.com/maps/ms?hl=en&gl=us&ptab=0&ie=UTF8&oe= UTF8&msa=0&msid=217262093643892057940.0004b931c8fd7fc649d3b&t=h&ll=39.9 89221,-75.19043&spn=0.12626,0.219727&z=12&source=embed (04/04/2013)

tor' that Black mobs were singling out random White people to beat up."[88]

It appears that *Southern Poverty Law Center* is far more interested in labeling conservative groups and people as "haters" than in classifying *all* racial hate crimes as hateful. This is the same group that labeled *Family Research Council* (FRC) a "hate group," which prompted a gay activist to take a loaded handgun (hidden inside a Chick-Fil-A bag) into FRC's headquarters in Washington, DC and open fire on a security guard when he attempted to stop him.[89]

The tragedy here is that so much of this has been inculcated by the politically correct left who seem to foment as much acrimony as possible as long as it is directed against *whites*. It is like they go out of their way to create problems for whites while excusing minorities.

This certainly seemed to be the case in the George Zimmerman and Trayvon Martin situation, where early on, Zimmerman was portrayed not as a Hispanic, but as a "white/Hispanic," which to my knowledge, had not been done before. That would be like referring to Obama as a "white/Arab," and I'm quite certain that many, including Mr. Obama himself, would be highly offended at that, given that he sees himself as black.

If there is fast becoming a true epidemic related to black on white crime, then it needs to be recognized *and* dealt with, but as we can see, too many are still ignoring it. In fact, even Mayor Nutter of Philadelphia ignored the facts for too long, stating in 2010 that *"there is*

---

[88] http://www.examiner.com/article/philadelphia-seen-as-major-hotspot-of-violent-hate-crimes (04/05/2013)
[89] http://www.dailymail.co.uk/news/article-2188889/Family-Research-Council-Gunman-carrying-bag-Chick-fil-A-goodies-opens—injuring-security-guard.html (04/05/2013)

no racial component"[90] to the crimes. This was in spite of the fact that blacks *were* (and still are) attacking whites.

Eventually, even Nutter was forced to admit what had become obvious. *"Things got so bad that Mayor Nutter reversed his claim on August 7th, 2011. He declared in a speech that the black perpetrators had brought, 'shame to their race.' He said the perpetrators were giving members of all races a reason to fear young black males. Nutter promised a curfew and a crackdown on his people."*[91]

Unfortunately, as the article goes on to state, things have not really improved. The tragedy here is that many of the young people involved in these specific crimes (some as young as 11 years old) think the entire thing is *funny*. While they beat whites, they are heard laughing and cracking jokes. Obviously, it's bad enough that people beat up strangers for the thrill of it, but to add insult to injury by treating the crime as if it's simply kids out for a joyride is an insult.

This is the fruit of *political correctness*. It simply pits one race, group, or class of people against another. Blacks are told repeatedly that the white man wants to hold them down. They believe the unproven critical race theory and react to it as if it is true.

Rev. Jesse Lee Peterson, in his book *SCAM*, tells us of an offshoot of the Nation of Islam (Farrakhan's group in the U.S.) called the *Five Percenters*. According to Peterson, *"The Five Percenters believe that the black man is 'God' and women are to be called 'Earth.' They also believe that they are the five percent of the population who are truly righteous and understand spiritual truths. Five percenters say that blacks are the original people of the earth, that they created civilization, and that whites ('devils') have deceived the world, causing people*

---

[90] http://www.examiner.com/article/philadelphia-seen-as-major-hotspot-of-violent-hate-crimes (04/05/2013)
[91] Ibid

to worship false gods. A number of hip-hop artists have been influenced by the Five Percenters, including Public Enemy, Ice Cube, Gang Starr, and others."[92]

Some of this became known to the press during the time following the arrests of John Muhammad and John Lee Malvo (Beltway Snipers), who drove around shooting mainly whites from the trunk of their car. Peterson states, *"The racial and political hatred that Muhammad and Malvo had for the United States was also apparently linked to...the 'Five Percenters'."*[93]

It seems that like the KKK, many of these black groups also traffic in racial hatred of others, especially whites. At the same time, they seem to have no problem cleaning their own house when it comes to dealing with other blacks who they see as becoming traitors to their cause.

"Malcolm X had been a mentor to Louis Farrakhan, who eventually replaced him as head of a Harlem Nation of Islam Temple. Malcolm X became viewed as a traitor to the Nation for openly discussing [Elijah] Muhammad's [previously known as Elijah Poole - ed.] adulterous affairs and for rejecting racism. Malcolm X began calling Muhammad a racist and a phony; the Nation's 'god' didn't appreciate the criticism. Upon learning of Malcolm X's betrayal, Muhammad told his followers, 'It's time to close that n*gger's eyes'."[94] Malcolm X was gunned down just days later.

In *SCAM*, Peterson also points out that the head of the Nation of Islam in America – Elijah Muhammad – *"hated America and loved its enemies...was also a serial adulterer who frequently had as many as seven*

---

[92] Rev. Jesse Lee Peterson *SCAM* (2003), pp. 121-122
[93] Ibid, p. 121
[94] Ibid, p. 118

different adulterous relationships going on at the same time...and sired thirteen children."[95]

We know that eventually, Louis Farrakhan took the reins of the Nation of Islam in America. Since that time, he has done what he can to portray the United States as an enemy of Islam and freedom. Eventually, because of his efforts, Libyan president Gadhafi pledged $1 billion *"to encourage minority political action in the U.S. According to Gadhafi, 'American blacks could set up their own state within the United States with the largest black army in the world.' Gadhafi also noted about Libya, 'Our confrontation with America used to be like confronting a fortress from outside. Today, we have found a loophole to enter the fortress and to confront it from with.'"*[96] It is no wonder that Farrakhan was so angry with Obama when Gadhafi's regime was overthrown.

There appears to be plenty of hatred emanating from certain black groups towards whites that is incited on a continual basis. It is something that should not be ignored, yet because of *political correctness*, it *is* ignored. We are all expected to turn a blind eye to it.

Something is obviously in the works. It would seem that some are working toward what can only be described as a race war. Peterson states, *"I consider Louis Farrakhan to be a serious threat to our national security and a subversive influence in our society. It is his theological belief that a race war is inevitable and that blacks will emerge victorious. He has political alignments with some of the world's most infamous terrorists, and his Nation of Islam is nothing less than an anti-American army that is poised to help destroy our nation.*

"I believe that if people do not wake up, and soon, we will have a race war in America – one that will cause bloodshed on a scale that we have

---

[95] Rev. Jesse Lee Peterson *SCAM* (2003), p. 117
[96] Ibid, p. 120

never seen before...Yet our nation's black preachers continue to ally themselves with this American Hitler. Their mutual hatred of whites and America is what links them together in their common cause against our nation."[97]

We need to remember that Rev. Jesse Lee Peterson is *black.* He moves and works among blacks and understands what is going on. The fact that white liberals exist who lie and rant against conservatives like Peterson is another cause for alarm. Either these individuals do not really know what they are doing, or they are trying to simply cover their tracks to give enough time for a race war to occur.

In any case, words from Holy Scripture about how bad things will become in these last days *are* coming true. The most we can do is prepare ourselves. I hope you are right with God. As Peter says, *"Therefore, prepare your minds for action, keep sober in spirit, fix your hope completely on the grace to be brought to you at the revelation of Jesus Christ"* (1 Peter 1:13).

---

[97] Rev. Jesse Lee Peterson *SCAM* (2003), p. 122

Chapter 14

Politically Correct Rules for Radicals

It is not difficult at all to see what has transpired in America (and much of the world) since Alinsky's *Rules for Radicals* was published in 1971 and taken to heart by the left as their mantra for world re-education and peace. Here are his rules.

1. *"Power is not only what you have, but what the enemy thinks you have."* Power is derived from two main sources – money and people; therefore, "Have-Nots" must build power from flesh and blood.

2. *"Never go outside the expertise of your people."* This results in confusion, fear and retreat. Feeling secure adds to the backbone of anyone.

3. *"Whenever possible, go outside the expertise of the enemy."* Look for ways to increase insecurity, anxiety and uncertainty.
4. *"Make the enemy live up to its own book of rules."* If the rule is that every letter gets a reply, send 30,000 letters. You can kill them with this because no one can possibly obey all of their own rules.
5. *"Ridicule is man's most potent weapon."* There is no defense. It's irrational. It's infuriating. It also works as a key pressure point to force the enemy into concessions.
6. *"A good tactic is one your people enjoy."* They'll keep doing it without urging and come back to do more. They're doing their thing, and will even suggest better ones.
7. *"A tactic that drags on too long becomes a drag."* Don't become old news.
8. *"Keep the pressure on. Never let up."* Keep trying new things to keep the opposition off-balance. As the opposition masters one approach, hit them from the flank with something new.
9. *"The threat is usually more terrifying than the thing itself."* Imagination and ego can dream up many more consequences than any activist.
10. *"The major premise for tactics is the development of operations that will maintain a constant pressure upon the opposition."* It is the unceasing pressure that will result in the reaction of the opposition that is essential for the success of the campaign.
11. *"If you push a negative hard enough, it will push through and become a positive."* Violence from the other side can win the public to your side because the public sympathizes with the underdog.
12. *"The price of a successful attack is a constructive alternative."* Never let the enemy score points because you're caught without a solution to the problem.
13. *"Pick the target, freeze it, personalize it, and polarize it."* Cut off the support network and isolate the target from sympathy. Go

after people and not institutions; people hurt faster than institutions.

Consider Rule #1. If something simply *appears* to be a majority, many will accept it as a *true* majority. The media tries hard to comply with this.

Rule #1 also implies a form of Marxism. The "have-nots" must become the "haves." They must have *power,* and in order to have that, they must take perceived power *away* from those who have it. The rest of the rules talk about how to do that.

Jump down to Rule #5. This is something that the left absolutely *excels* in. We witnessed it live with the debate (such as it was) between Joe Biden and Paul Ryan, during which Biden used facial expressions as well as words to *ridicule* Ryan. Notice that Alinsky states that using ridicule has no defense because he admits that it is *irrational.*

We listen to some political pundit spend three to five minutes panning someone like Dr. Ben Carson and they might *eventually* get into actually presenting a fact. A person responding to it has two options: join in the ridicule or ignore it by treating it as if it does not exist. The latter option gets tiring quickly.

Ridicule is what is used on the child's playground when insults fly vehemently back and forth between two children who are not capable of actually dealing with facts. This tells us a good deal about the left.

One morning I was watching Chris Matthews and he was on a kick about Sarah Palin. As he introduced the subject, he insulted her no less than five times. He started out by calling Palin a "balloon head." Remember when sticks and stones could break bones, but names could never hurt you? The left never got that memo.

Rule #8 is also interesting: *keeping the pressure up*. During the "Fast and Furious" and "Benghazi" situations, the media that are firmly in bed with the left kept the pressure up, but on *who*? They went into attack mode against anyone who dared question the Obama administration. Instead of doing their level best to get all the facts, they simply resorted to pressuring people who *wanted* the facts by charging them with "politicizing" the situation. When that didn't work, they fell back on the one thing that had worked and played the race card. The left is like some huge bouncer that has only one job – to keep you away from the club.

You notice how much these events are in the news *now*, right? They're *not,* and anyone who brings them up is accused of racism, politics, or both. Many of us would like to see *justice*, but that's too much to ask, apparently. Political correctness does not seek justice. It seeks "equality" and "freedom" and it uses the race card often to achieve it.

This has nothing to do with journalistic integrity and everything to do with Alinsky's methods for those who wish to radicalize people of America for Marxist change. For the longest time, every honest question from conservatives was simply met with *"You're a racist!"* by the left. The fact that they created this protective wall around Obama and his administration simply made folks think all the more that something was being hidden.

Rule #9 is funny. We heard "sequester" as if it was the largest demon one can imagine, hiding just off stage in the shadows. Under no circumstances did we want to allow that demon to gain center stage! Sequester. It's *bad*. It will mean this, that, and the other thing as America heads over the fiscal cliff.

We finally have sequester and what has happened? Not much. Certainly, Obama acts as if there is no sequester. He's released $500 million to the Middle East that had been frozen by Congress. Can he do that? No one is asking the question as it's probably considered "racist," though just the other day he stated he was "constrained" by the Constitution with respect to the 2nd Amendment. Really? I don't believe he actually believes that, but time will tell.

Obama continues to have ultra-expensive parties at the White House "mansion," but is "forced" to close White House tours because of sequester even after people offer to pay for them. The DHS spends $50 million on new uniforms, buys over a billion dollars' worth of ammo, spends millions for lightweight armored tanks and scarfs up 7,000 AR (good defensive) weapons.

It's a joke really. Alinsky was right. Talking up sequester made it appear worse than it actually is when all is said and done. But we still have three more years of Obama's tax and spend policies, though little to nothing is actually spent here in America to help create jobs.

Rule #11 is also interesting and we saw this at work with the unions and their "struggles" last year. Unfortunately, people have lost sympathy for unions because of the thug tactics they use. Darn. Of course, it also helps when the media portrays unions as only wanting what's best for employees, even if that means that businesses like Hostess wind up closing their doors. Hey, where is the unions' concern for those employees now?

Rule #13 was employed during the George Zimmerman/Trayvon Martin shooting aftermath. Zimmerman was the isolated target cut off from sympathy. He was portrayed as a "white/Hispanic" in order to incite blacks against whites. MSNBC deliberately edited audio/video on at least two separate occasions to portray Zimmerman in a negative (and untruthful) light. The goal was to pump up Martin in spite of what may have actually transpired during that encounter. I'm *glad* Zimmerman is suing. I cannot imagine him getting a fair trial, though, I'm afraid.

The press essentially *charged* Zimmerman, found him *guilty*, and then called for his execution (by printing a story of the New Black Panthers and their offer of money for Zimmerman – *dead* or *alive* – prior to his arrest). The public was whipped up, and of course, Al Sharpton played his part in the debacle as well. The left can always count on that racist to foment ill will toward whites.

The media went even further by obviously Photoshopping pictures of Martin to make him appear less of a thug. They never printed the photos of Martin from his own social network page showing him double flipping off the viewer with low-hanging pants. The only photos they showed were in his football uniform and those of that nature. But of course, the media also had no problem doctoring photos of Zimmerman so that cuts and bruises on his nose and back of head could not be seen.

Yet, even though we have many examples of how the media *lies* because of their left-leaning bias, there are still people who say, *"Bias? What bias?"* when it comes to the media. When they are not being biased, they are simply admitting what they do not know, as in the case of a commentator on CBS recently stating that John the Baptist was at the crucifixion of Jesus.[98] Yes, they corrected that later, but a bit of research ahead of time on their part would have eliminated the error before it occurred. Maybe they meant John's *ghost*.

There's a lot more to Alinsky than simply these rules as listed. It's all in his book and I suggest purchasing it, if for no other reason than to know what the left's playbook is all about.

---

[98] http://pjmedia.com/tatler/2013/04/04/cbs-hey-john-the-baptist-attended-jesus-crucifixion/ (04/05/2013)

It seems to me that the left has been working overtime to prevent true dialogue for one reason. They know that the facts are not on their side, so they ignore the facts and go for the proverbial jugular. It's easier. It's also better for ratings if you happen to have a radio or TV show. I'm really surprised that outright lying was not specifically one of Alinsky's rules, although it is implied in several of them.

Remember, Alinsky is the guy who threw a high-five to "Lucifer" in his book. He thought it was great that Lucifer (Satan) had enough guts to stand up to God and because of it received his own kingdom. Of course, what Alinsky pays no attention to is that Satan's kingdom is very *temporary*. He won't always be the god of this world.

Had Satan not stood up to God and then inserted himself as the prime reason for humanity's fall, Satan would also not be currently bound up in the same limitation that humanity suffers from: *time*. Whether he likes it or not, Satan is bound by the same laws of time that we are bound by. At some point in *time*, his kingdom will end and he will reap the rewards of his treachery.

Satan, Alinsky, and too many others can then spend their respective eternities discussing what went wrong and why Satan was not powerful enough to overcome the very God he stood up to in the first place. For that matter, neither was Alinsky.

Chapter 15

Politically Correct Race War and Reparations

Yep. I know. The title of this chapter is certainly nothing that intelligent people want to discuss. It moves into the area of *conspiracy* and we all know too well that conspiracy theorists wear tin hats and say and believe things that defy logic and reason.

But some things need to be said and at least considered. Previously, we quoted several people who have become known as leaders within conservative circles, who also happen to be black. They speak of things that have affected the black community in a very negative way.

Rev. Jesse Lee Peterson speaks of the fact that Louis Farrakhan is someone who hates America and white people. I've quoted from Colin Flaherty, who has written about the black and white crime that is growing throughout many places in America.

Since Obama took office and in spite of the fact that his administration was to be the most transparent one in history and that he would do what he could to heal the division between races, he has not lived up to those promises. If anything, problems between races have increased, and at least some of that has to do with the racist policies of Eric Holder's so-called Department of Justice. Obama himself has taken pains to hide many things about himself and the daily workings of his own administration. Far from being transparent, he is extremely secretive.

One author states, "*This nation is poised for a battle that will divide us like never before. We have reaped destruction from welfare, affirmative action, Rodney King and the L.A. riots, and O.J. Simpson, but there is one battle that I'm afraid we may not recover from as a nation. That battle is for slavery 'reparations'.*"[99]

These words are from Rev. Jesse Lee Peterson, a black leader who is routinely criticized by the left because he is not in step with their agenda. Peterson further states, "*The whole idea of reparations is racist and divisive in and of itself. It is racist in that it unfairly burdens white America with the mistakes of the past – mistakes they had nothing to do with! It is divisive because it foments rage that should have been discarded years ago. In short, the reparations movement is just another misuse of the slavery issue by the civil rights establishment to gain power and wealth.*"[100]

If we stop to consider that these words come from the pen of an intelligent, conservative, black leader, we then have to stop and won-

---

[99] Rev. Jesse Lee Peterson *SCAM* (2003), p. 69
[100] Ibid, p. 69

127

der how and why people like Al Sharpton, Jesse Jackson, and too many others like them do not feel the same way. Why is their hatred of white America allowed to grow to the point where their demands for reparations are actually seen as an intelligent response to a problem that occurred generations ago in this country and no one living today ever owned a slave or was a slave?

Maybe the problem is not so much that these individuals want reparations for blacks in general. Maybe the problem is in what they themselves can get out of the system for their own advantage.

"During the last forty years, black leaders in this country seem to have grown in wealth, power, and fame, while the grievances and complaints of average black Americans have only worsened. What we need to realize is that these leaders are not working for the black community, but against it. By keeping blacks enraged at whites, their status continues to grow. But if blacks were to give up their rage, these 'leaders' would no longer be necessary. That is why they drum up insidious ideas such as reparations – a plot of which, I believe, will be the most destructive blacks have ever faced."[101]

Peterson asks who would pay these reparations and he answers his own question by stating that it would be the people who do not have a racist bone in their body and immigrated to this country well after the Civil War took place. He also notes that black taxpayers would also be part of that process. They would, in essence, be paying their own reparations.

Peterson affirms that *"White America is not guilty of the sins of the past, and they must be careful not to fall to the anger of these socialist, destructive black leaders who want to racially divide and conquer us. Black Americans must drop their anger and realize that it is not the*

---

[101] Rev. Jesse Lee Peterson *SCAM* (2003), pp. 69-70

white American who is causing their destruction but their own so-called leaders, whose evil machinations know no end."[102]

Of course, if these leaders were to do what Peterson is demanding, they would, in essence, be out of a job. If they stopped inciting anger among blacks, if they stopped leading their own personal revolutions against white America, and if they ceased their anger-filled torrents of racist diatribes against white Americans, they would have absolutely nothing to do, would they?

It is their anger that keeps them going. It is their anger that prompts their actions. Sadly, both Sharpton and Jackson have the initials "Rev" in front of their names. We are to believe that they are Christian as they whip up the troops into a frenzy-filled hatred of white Americans. The only whites they can stomach are those who are filled with the same type of loathing for other whites. However, when push comes to shove, these black leaders would dump their white, liberal "friends" quicker than a fox can outrun a chicken.

Ultimately, the only people these black leaders care about are themselves and they are *using* the black community for their own personal gain and privilege. It is no different from what Margaret Sanger did when she became associated with the Rockefellers and their eugenics program. The desire was to rid the earth of what were believed to be "unfit" individuals and that included (for Sanger) those of the "Negro" race. We'll get into her life soon.

Rev. Peterson relates in his September 1, 2012 newsletter from BOND, *"Twenty-five years ago, when God took away the anger I harbored for my parent' failings, many things about me changed. One was that I ceased being a liberal Democrat and became a conservative Republican. That bothered my family! Though my family disagreed with*

---

[102] Rev. Jesse Lee Peterson *SCAM* (2003), p. 71

me, they respect me, because through my new maturity I've helped many of them with their challenges."

Yet what is troublesome is the amount of *white* (especially *young*) people who are avowed *liberals* and who also call themselves Christian. I'm not judging them as to the validity of their Christianity. I'm simply saying that as far as I can see, Jesus does not agree with the Democratic Party. After all, most of them booed when they voted to add "God" back into the platform at the Democratic National Convention in 2012. Not only that, but most are also pro-choice, which really means pro-murder in this case since abortion stops a beating heart and it is done intentionally.

There is very little (if anything) within the liberal policies of the left that mirror biblical Christianity, yet you can't tell this to young people who claim Jesus as Lord and Savior. They know everything and believe that because they are "helping" poor and underprivileged (by keeping them on the "plantation" as Ben Carson and others would say), then they are living Christianity. It's simply not true, but they obviously do not see that. Unfortunately for these folks, when you take the time to really compare biblical truth with the policies of the left, there is little, if any, commonality.

Getting back to the issue of reparations, Peterson asks where the idea came from in the first place. *"As you might expect, the absurd idea of paying blacks for the sins of slaveholders more than 150 years ago comes from the fevered minds of socialists and racist Afrocentrists who hate America and whites. Today, this whole idea of reparations is being headed by racist leaders of the black community such as Randall Robinson, former executive director of TransAfrica Forum and author of The Debt: What America Owes to Blacks. It is also being pushed by U.S. Representative John Conyers (D-Michigan), who, since 1989, has unsuccessfully presented legislation calling for a study on reparations; Leonard Jeffries, a racist political science professor; and Ebony magazine Editor Lerone Bennett Jr.*

"These are just a few of the black liberal 'leaders' who would rather keep blacks angry than demonstrate to them how they themselves have become successful in life. As the rest of the black community is going to hell, these men are becoming wealthy and powerful and are not think-ing twice about us. If – God forbid – blacks were to receive so-called reparations, I am convinced that this money would end up in the hands of these black leaders, politicians, and lawyers, as well as many of the black ministers. In addition to solving nothing, reparations would only fuel the anger of the black community because reparations would be another failure – just as affirmative action and welfare have been."[103]

If, by "failure," Peterson means that programs like affirmative action and welfare have not *benefitted* the black community, then he's abso-lutely correct. Many within the black community have become ac-customed to receiving these entitlements and learned they are "owed" something by whites. However, as far as racist, liberal whites are concerned, these programs have been an outstanding success be-cause it keeps blacks "on the plantation" and therefore controlled.

Of course, it needs to stop. There are plenty of blacks in communities who want to be free of government-sponsored poverty. They want the government to simply provide funds, expertise, and people to help improve their living conditions, as a place to start. They will then be able to move away from the cycle of poverty that exists for them. This is certainly reasonable and it is something our govern-ment should be doing. Yet this same government apparently doesn't have enough money to go around after sending millions and billions of American dollars *overseas* to help Egypt, Libya, or some other for-eign government.

Our government wants to keep blacks "in their place." They believe that simply *giving* them welfare and other entitlements will pull the wool over their eyes into thinking they are self-sufficient. In truth,

---

[103] Rev. Jesse Lee Peterson *SCAM* (2003), pp. 71-72

our government continues the practice (started in earnest under Lyndon B. Johnson) of keeping blacks *enslaved*. They have hand-picked racist blacks who do the bidding of their white, racist "masters," who do their part to keep the blindfolds securely over the eyes of the black community; otherwise they might wake up to the truth, as Rev. Jesse Lee Peterson has done.

Chapter 16

Politically Correct Racism of Margaret Sanger

As far as Planned Parenthood founder Margaret Sanger was concerned, *all* black babies should be aborted, along with other children from races who were not of the highest stock. In a 1939 memo to Dr. Clarence J. Gamble (of Proctor & Gamble), Sanger stated, "**We do not want the word to go out that we want to exterminate the Negro population**, *and the minister is the man who can straighten that idea out if it ever occurs to any of their more rebellious members.*"[104] This was in response to Gamble's memo to Sanger about something he had come up with to eradicate blacks, in what he called "Suggestion for Negro Project." (emphasis added)

---

[104] http://www.blackgenocide.org/sanger02.html (04/05/2013)

Please do not lose sight of the fact that Sanger specifically stated that they wanted to *exterminate* blacks but did *not* want that to become *known* by the general black population. Hence, the idea to use black ministers to hide the fact that the ulterior motive involved *eliminating* the black race was what Gamble had come up with, to which Sanger agreed.

The racist history of Planned Parenthood is something those on the left dutifully ignore. In an attempt to "prove" that the group is free of racism, Faye Wattleton was appointed as the group's president from 1978 to 1992 and was the first black woman to hold the post.

Of course, feminists and others on the left go out of their way in their attempts to destroy the notion that Sanger was a racist. They go so far as to admit to the fact that she was a *eugenicist*. While that's not great either, it's certainly better than being a racist. Unfortunately, the facts prove otherwise.

With respect to alleged racist statements by Sanger, they are often met with claims of her comments being taken out of context. Noting the statement, *"We do not want the word to get out that we want to exterminate the Negro population,"* it is said that the comment – by itself – can *seem* to appear racist, but after closer examination, it is not.

"Margaret Sanger was aware of concerns that birth control would pose a threat to the African American community. Consequently, she was determined to alleviate these concerns by involving the African American community in the formation of birth control clinics in the South. The quote above comes from a letter that Sanger wrote to Dr. Clarence J. Gamble, one of the financial backers of the birth control movement. In the letter, Sanger argued that African American doctors needed to be employed at birth control clinics. Sanger felt that it was important to employ black doctors and social workers in order for patients to feel that the clinics represented their community. When the Birth Control

Federation of America became Planned Parenthood Federation of America in 1942, Sanger established the Division of Negro Service to oversee outreach to the African American community nationally. Sanger's work was endorsed by African American leaders, such as Martin Luther King, Jr. and W.E.B. DuBois."[105]

Birth control itself was not the concern. Forced *sterilization* was the concern, but note how the quote simply references "birth control."

It can be *clearly* shown that many of the early eugenicists in America were Nazis who simply brought over their supremacy of the white race to America. Of course, we'll also show that the above quote contains fallacies that are presented as fact.

The person we've quoted is lying. Sanger *did* "reach out" to the African American community. However, it was *not* for the purposes implied in the above quote. We will show that initially, those in the black community grew concerned that Sanger's clinics were merely covers for forced sterilization of blacks.

"Margaret Sanger aligned herself with the eugenicists whose ideology prevailed in the early 20th century. Eugenicists strongly espoused racial supremacy and 'purity,' particularly of the 'Aryan' race. Eugenicists hoped to purify the bloodlines and improve the race by encouraging the 'fit' to reproduce and the 'unfit' to restrict their reproduction. They sought to contain the 'inferior' races through segregation, sterilization, birth control and abortion."[106]

The more the subject of eugenics is studied, the more the reality of its racist intents becomes obvious. The left cannot admit this, though, because it plays against their agenda.

Some of the sentiments expressed by Sanger include the following:

---

[105] http://feministsforchoice.com/was-margaret-sanger-a-racist.htm (04/05/2013)
[106] http://www.cwfa.org/articledisplay.asp?id=1466 (04/05/2013)

"[Slavs, Latin, and Hebrew immigrants are] human weeds ... a dead weight of human waste ... [Blacks, soldiers, and Jews are a] menace to the race."[107]

Commenting on Australian Aborigines, Sanger noted, *"The lower down in the scale of human development we go the less sexual control we find. It is said the aboriginal Australian, the lowest known species of the human family, just a step higher than the chimpanzee in brain development, has so little sexual control that police authority alone prevents him from obtaining sexual satisfaction on the streets. According to one writer, the rapist has just enough brain development to raise him above the animal, but like the animal, when in heat, knows no law except nature, which impels him to procreate, whatever the result."*[108]

Much of the eugenics movement based polices on one of Margaret Sanger's books, *The Pivot of Civilization*. A free, downloadable copy is available at the link below.[109] Read it to be enlightened.

One author, in describing Sanger's penchant for doing all she could to reduce the birth of blacks and Hispanics, noted how she began to set up shop in those communities. *"As her organization grew, Sanger set up more clinics in the communities of other 'dysgenic races'—such as Blacks and Hispanics. Sanger turned her attention to 'Negroes' in 1929 and opened another clinic in Harlem in 1930. Sanger, 'in alliance with eugenicists, and through initiatives such as the Negro Project ... exploited black stereotypes in order to reduce the fertility of African Americans.' The all-white staff and the sign identifying the clinic as a 'research bureau' raised the suspicions of the black community. They feared that the clinic's actual goal was to 'experiment on and sterilize black people'. Their fears were not unfounded: Sanger once addressed the women's branch of the Klu Klux Klan in Silver Lake, New Jersey, and*

---

[107] Margaret Sanger, April 1933 Birth Control Review

[108] Sanger, M.H., *What Every Girl Should Know*, Belvedere Publishers, New York, p. 40, 1980. A reprint of the original 1920 edition.

[109] http://www.gutenberg.org/ebooks/1689 (04/06/2013)

received a 'dozen invitations to speak to similar groups'. Flynn claims that she was on good terms with other racist organizations."[110]

Unlike what our friend from the Feminists for Choice website believes (as quoted previously), it was not birth control that caused concern. It was something more reprehensible that caused those within the black communities to stay away. If Sanger *was* involved in forced involuntary sterilization of people she did not believe should be allowed to procreate, then she had set herself up as God. This is what eugenicists do. Euthanasia is also part and parcel of the eugenics movement.

Realizing there was a problem, Sanger did what she could to alleviate suspicions among the black populace. *"Sanger believed the 'Negro district' was the 'headquarters for the criminal element' and concluded that, as the title of a book by a member of her board proclaimed, The Rising Tide of Color Against White World Supremacy, was a rise that had to be stemmed. To deal with the problem of resistance among the black population, Sanger recruited black doctors, nurses, ministers and social workers 'in order to gain black patients' trust' in order 'to limit or even erase the black presence in America'."*[111]

Sanger had it all figured out apparently. She used other blacks who knowingly or unknowingly worked to assuage fears in the black community. This then allowed them to take advantage of the "birth control" that was being offered through Sanger's research bureaus.

Yet today, the group she formed – Planned Parenthood – has done whatever possible to hide this true history from the public. Yes, they'll admit that eugenics in and of itself is *not* a good thing (though

---

[110] Flynn, D.J., *Intellectual Morons: How Ideology Makes Smart People Fall for Stupid Ideas*, Crown Forum, New York, 2004., p. 153

[111] Washington, H.A., *Medical Apartheid: The Dark History of Medical Experimentation on Black Americans from Colonial Times to the Present*, Doubleday, New York, pp. 197-198, 2006.

it is *still* done), but Sanger was merely a woman of her time. By no means was Margaret Sanger a racist, they argue. The actual facts prove differently, but few are interested in actual truth today.

*"The term 'eugenics' was first used in 1883 by Francis Galton, Darwin's half cousin. In 1871, Darwin authored the racist book The Descent of Man and Selection in Relation to Sex saying that '***the civilized races of man will almost certainly exterminate, and replace, the savage races*** throughout the world.' This followed the principle of 'survival of the fittest' coined by Herbert Spencer in 1864 after reading Darwin's 1959 book, The Origin of the Species by Means of Natural Selection for the Preservation of Favored Races in the Struggle for Life (four years after Arthur Gobineau's An Essay on the Inequality of the Races). For humans, this principle expressed itself in Social Darwinism."*[112] (emphasis added)

Most people are completely unaware of the racist leanings of Darwin, and those who *are* aware of it do their best to cast it off as merely an anomaly of those who lived during that time. Again, this is completely untrue, but truth has little use to those on the left who do their best to reimagine history as often as possible.

Because of the godlessness of Darwinism, eugenics became a natural byproduct of it. What people fail to realize is that eugenics is the direct involvement of science on people, for the express purpose of fine tuning (as it were) the human race. This is done by culling out those thought to be "inferior."

May I again refer you to the section of the text I have bolded in the previous quote? Who is going to *"exterminate, and replace, the savage races..."*? According to the quote, it is the *"civilized races of man"* that will do that. This pits one race (the "superior") against the rest ("inferior" races).

---

[112] Dennis L. Cuddy *New World Order: The Rise of Techno-Feudalism* (2010), p. 153

Dr. Dennis Cuddy, in his book *New World Order: The Rise of Techno-Feudalism*, shows how this belief started with Darwinism, and by the 1870s, it was being taught in the halls of Oxford by people like John Ruskin. Interestingly enough, one of Ruskin's students was none other than Cecil Rhodes (who eventually went on to form the *Rhodes Scholarship* and was also a member of *Skull & Bones*).

Young minds were taught that they were the best and brightest and their blood was noble blood. They were destined to rule over all other races. That was their calling and they should take it seriously.

Cuddy also points out that in the early 1900s, Madame Blavatsky and her *Theosophical Society* had been instilled with the "*Aryan doctrine [that] had spread through Germany and Austria, and it was from her writings that a young Adolph Hitler learned the meaning of the Aryan swastika.*"[113]

Cuddy connects the dots for us to show how these same ideas developed in America. It was through individuals like Andrew Carnegie and John Rockefeller who "*played an important part in funding the eugenics movement. In 1904, the Carnegie Institution, with Skull & Bones member Daniel Coit Gilman as president, financed the establishment of a biological experiment station related to eugenics at Cold Spring Harbor, New York. In 1910, the Eugenics Record Office was begun there and later received funding from the Rockefeller Foundation after John D. Rockefeller, Jr. formed the Bureau of Social Hygiene.*"[114]

So what does all this have to do with Margaret Sanger? As Cuddy points out, "*It was during this time of the early twentieth century that Rockefeller introduced Margaret Sanger to the monied elite who would help her form the Birth Control League which would later become Planned Parenthood. The November 1921 issue of Sanger's Birth Control Review carried the heading 'Birth Control: To Create a Race of*

---

[113] Cuddy *New World Order: The Rise of Techno-Feudalism* (2010), pp. 153-154
[114] Ibid, p. 154

Thoroughbreds,' and Sanger would later advocate eugenically limiting 'dysgenic stocks' such as blacks, Hispanics, American Indians, and Catholics, as well as 'slum dwellers' such as Jewish immigrants."[115]

It seems that "Nazism" with its accompanying Aryan race philosophies was in America before Hitler became a household name. What is interesting is the fact that by the time the *"April 1933 edition of Margaret Sanger's Birth Control Review [was published], Dr. Ernst Rudin of Hitler's Nazi Third Reich wrote 'Eugenic Sterilization: An Urgent Need'."*[116]

But of course, eugenics died with Hitler and Sanger, right? Think again. Part of the Nazi plan was the selection of the "inferior" races for extermination. This was directed mainly at Jewish people, since they had been the "chosen people," but it was believed that God had fully rejected them. This is why Hitler felt compelled to rid the earth of Jews. They are a fallen, cast away people. There is nothing left for them anymore since they rejected the Messiah in Jesus and sent him to Roman authorities to be executed.

What Hitler did by killing millions of Jews, he thought it right. He believed God blessed his efforts. By the way, Replacement Theology allows and encourages this anti-Semitic attitude because it erroneously states that God is done with the Jews and all remaining promises have been transferred to the Church. I've spoken with many Replacement theologians and it amazes me how *angry* they get when they speak of "the Jews."

But Hitler did *not* kill just Jewish people. Hitler executed anyone whom he believed was unfit to live. To his way of thinking, white Anglo-Saxons were the elite of all the races. Anyone not of Aryan blood *could* be executed. This actually speeded up the evolutionary

---

[115] Ibid, pp. 154-155
[116] Cuddy *New World Order: The Rise of Techno-Feudalism* (2010), p. 155

process, as far as Hitler was concerned. He was simply helping "God" get the human race to its pre-appointed conclusion sooner.

Did Germany's defeat and Hitler's death destroy the philosophy that guided the Nazis? *"[W]hen Fabian Socialist Sir Julian Huxley became the first director-general of UNESCO (United Nations Educational, Scientific and Cultural Organization), he authored UNESCO: Its Purpose and Its Philosophy (1948) in which he revealed that 'even though it is quite true that any radical eugenic policy will be for many years politically and psychologically impossible, it will be important for UNESCO to see that the eugenic problem is examined with the greatest care, and that the public mind is informed of the issues at stake so that much that is now unthinkable may at least become thinkable.'*

"This was three years after the founding of the Human Betterment League in 1945 in North Carolina, one of the leading states in forced sterilization (in the late 1970s, Dr. Harmon Smith of Duke University said North Carolina had one of the most thorough involuntary sterilization programs in the U.S.). The league's director was Alice Shelton Gray who worked with **Margaret Sanger***. Gray was succeeded as league director by C. Nash Herndon (Carnegie fellow, 1940-41), who became president of the American Eugenics Society from 1952 to 1955."*[117] (emphasis added)

There is a continuum that carries eugenics through to today. It includes people like Barbara Marx Hubbard, who is well known in New Age circles. In her book *The Book of Co-Creation*, she states, *"Out of the full spectrum of human personality, one-fourth is electing to transcend...one-fourth is destructive [and] they are defective seeds...[who] must be eliminated from the social body."*[118] Notice that Hubbard states that one-fourth of humans are "defective" and will need to be destroyed. How will that occur? As Hubbard states, "we" (meaning

---

[117] Dennis L. Cuddy *New World Order: The Rise of Techno-Feudalism* (2010), p. 156
[118] Ibid, p. 157

her and those who believe as she does) are given the task by God of *completing* the selection process ("He selects, we destroy") and she identifies her group as those of the Pale Horse, *death*.

For anyone who has studied the tenets and teachings of those leaders within the New Age, the truth becomes clear. Many on earth are destined for destruction by being singled out from the rest.

This is why Roe v. Wade will likely *never* be overturned. Abortion on demand is too much a part of the eugenics program that goes all the way back to Darwin and became firmly ensconced in American society through the efforts of people like Margaret Sanger.

Chapter 17

Politically Correct Screams of Death

My son and I went to a local Mexican restaurant for dinner one evening while my wife was out of town. There was no point trying to cook for ourselves, though my son is a decent cook. While sitting in the booth, waiting for our food, I glanced at the TV overhead to catch the local news.

We were there for probably an hour, eating chips and salsa, drinking some diet soda (I know, it's bad for you), and then we ate our food once it arrived. I'm glad we went.

On the news, I saw everything from an interview with Tiger Woods from the current Masters golf tournament at Augusta, to brush fires in the West, to snow drifts in the Midwest, to a tale of a family that had kidnapped their two sons and run off to Cuba, to other things in between. I even listened to a bit of news about political website *Mother Jones* and the accusation that they bugged Mitch McConnell's office and overheard his plans of how to take care of actress Ashley Judd when it looked like she was planning a run for his seat.

However, one thing I did *not* see was anything related to abortion practitioner Kermit Gosnell and his alleged "house of horrors" clinic. Not a peep.

Yet there had been dramatic and even *traumatic* testimony from at least one worker the day before in Philadelphia. Abortion clinic employee Sherry West spoke of how she heard the "screams" of a child who was aborted and survived. West stated that the child sounded like an alien. West told the judge *"that the body of the child was about 18 to 24 inches long and was one of the largest babies she had seen delivered during abortion procedures at Gosnell's clinic."*[119]

Can you imagine how many times West will relive *that* sound in her head? I cannot imagine hearing the screams from a child that was supposed to have *died* during the abortion process, but *lived*, screaming itself to death. *"West said she saw the child, whose face and features were not yet completely formed, lying on a glass tray on a shelf and she told a co-worker to call Gosnell about it and fled the room."*[120]

I am at a loss. I simply do *not* understand. How is this *not* murder? How can people do this to other *people*? Where is the outrage from Hollywood? Where is Jim Carrey to call abortion doctors "mother "f*ckers" like he did gun owners? Where is the constant pa-

---

[119] http://www.lifenews.com/2013/04/08/gosnell-worker-baby-screamed-during-live-birth-abortion/ (05/22/2013)
[120] Ibid

rade of celebrities stepping up to the microphone to condemn the killing of unborn children? Nothing but silence.

Many on Twitchy wonder why the news is not covering it at all.

It's a good question to ask. I guess it's more important to get the latest from Tiger Woods than to learn exactly what went on in the horror shop of Kermit Gosnell.[121]

It might also do well to ask where Obama is regarding this. He has had little problem inserting himself into other situations where blacks were victims or when he personally has an interest in something like gun control.

Recall the case of a black college professor who was arrested for what seemed to be breaking into a vacant house and Obama's statement that the police may have overreacted. We also know what Obama said with respect to the tragedy surrounding the Zimmerman/Martin situation. Yet, in the case of Beyonce and Jay-Z vacationing in apartheid Cuba (with plenty of blacks treated as 3rd class citizens there with indefinite stays in jail) or the murderous exploits of Kermit Gosnell, Obama's pet crickets speak for him.

Like Obama, the mainstream news is silent about this latest testimony related to Gosnell's inhumanity. They would likely provide some excuse about not wanting to create a situation that may prejudice people against Gosnell. No, it's more likely they do not want to publicize the terrible problems associated with abortion.

Look, the left's agenda is very clear. When it comes to abortion, the right of women to murder on demand *must* be protected.

---

[121] http://twitchy.com/2013/04/09/baby-screamed-media-silent-the-msm-blackout-on-news-of-gosnell-worker-who-heard-newborn-screaming/ (05/22/2013)

According to *political correctness*, women are "victims," and as such, must be accorded every opportunity to level the playing field. If this means making it legally permissible for women to kill their unborn children, so be it.

Gosnell *"faces 43 criminal counts, including eight counts of murder in the death of one patient, Karnamaya Monger, and seven newborn infants. Additional charges include conspiracy, drug delivery resulting in death, infanticide, corruption of minors, evidence tampering, theft by deception, abuse of corpse, and corruption."*[122]

I'm at a bit of a loss here. Gosnell is an *abortionist*. He *kills* unborn children for a living. Why is he being charged with the deaths of seven newborn infants and infanticide? Aren't these considered *late-term abortions*, when their necks are cut *as* they exit the womb?

Oh wait, they must magically go from "specimen" (not viable) to "baby" (viable) once they *leave* the womb. How stupid of me not to realize the difference, nuanced though it may be.

I cannot imagine for one second that God sees a difference. Abortion is *murder* and thou shalt not *murder* (kill).

Not only have we made murder accessible, but we have made it completely *acceptable*. Woe to us.

---

[122] http://www.lifenews.com/2013/04/08/gosnell-worker-baby-screamed-during-live-birth-abortion/ (05/22/2013)

Chapter 18

Politically Correct Gun Confiscation

When he can use it to his advantage, Obama refers to the Constitution. To allay fears, he recently stated that he is *"constrained…by a system that our Founders put in place. It's a government of and by and for the people."*[123] These are very true words. Hear, hear.

This was stated while Obama was in Colorado with a group of police officers as a backdrop prop. The comments reflect his own admission

---

[123] http://washington.cbslocal.com/2013/04/04/obama-i-am-constrained-by-a-system-that-our-founders-put-in-place/ (04/10/2013)

that the government cannot simply come in and take a law-abiding citizen's legally owned gun away from him/her. It was Obama's way of pooh-poohing the idea that some believe we *"need a gun to protect [ourselves] from the government."*[124]

We've also heard Biden say that nothing the federal government is trying to do will infringe on the 2nd Amendment. Unfortunately, this is leftist speak (a lie) because every time the government adds more laws to the books that have to do with buying guns or ammo, they are infringing on the 2nd Amendment. They do not see it that way, of course.

However, *saying* something and *meaning* it are two different things. The natural question in response to Obama's statement is this: *does he really mean and believe what he says?* We have no honest way of knowing *for now*.

Because Obama has (like most politicians) either stretched the truth or outright lied so often (true leftist speak), we honestly cannot know what his intentions are until time passes to *see* what will happen. It remains an open-ended question.

But, while Obama is telling us that *he* is constrained by a specific system that protects law-abiding citizens from government overreach, other Democrats don't seem to share that same sentiment. I'm referring to Cuomo and other Democrat governors who see no difficulty in passing illegal laws in their state that either go *up to* or *include* gun confiscation.

In fact, in case you haven't heard, Gov. Cuomo (D-NY) actually used the word *"confiscation"* in referring to new gun control laws shortly after the Sandy Hook tragedy. His exact words on a radio program

---

[124] http://washington.cbslocal.com/2013/04/04/obama-i-am-constrained-by-a-system-that-our-founders-put-in-place/ (04/10/2013)

were, *"Confiscation could be an option. Mandatory sale to the state could be an option. Permitting could be an option — keep your gun but permit it."*[125]

My question is, if Obama says *he* is constrained by the system, why isn't Cuomo *also* constrained by this same system? Obama's words actually point to the illegalities of Cuomo's words and resultant actions. Moreover, as of this writing, I am not aware that Obama has stepped up to the plate to point out that Cuomo is *wrong* in the direction he is headed with respect to gun control, have you?

We have Obama saying he is constrained. Cuomo says gun confiscation could be an option. Obama has not publicly corrected Cuomo.

But the other question is this: has Cuomo made good on his potential threat to confiscate guns? Why *yes*, he *has*.

According to The Blaze, Cuomo has – in fact – begun taking away guns from law-abiding citizens. *"On April 1st, a legal gun owner in upstate New York reportedly received an official notice from the state ordering him to surrender any and all weapons to his local police department. The note said that the person's permit to own a gun in New York was being suspended as well. The gun owner contacted attorney Jim Tresmond (a specialist in gun laws in New York) and the two visited the local police precinct."*[126] The guns were turned over and the gun owner was given a receipt for the items.

This is patently *illegal*. The government cannot simply force law-abiding citizens with no criminal record to turn their guns over to law enforcement, yet it *is* happening, in spite of Obama saying that it

---

[125] http://hotair.com/archives/2012/12/22/confiscation-could-be-an-option/ (04/10/2013)
[126] http://www.theblaze.com/stories/2013/04/09/a-form-of-gun-confiscation-has-reportedly-begun-in-new-york-state-heres-the-justification-being-used/ (04/10/2013)

cannot happen. The question then is how *did* this happen, and has it happened more than once?

Apparently, the gun owner in question had a *"short-term health issue that required medication."*[127] The man's lawyer is trying to determine *how* and *by whom* that information was forwarded on to the authorities from healthcare providers.

Under the recently approved *NY Safe Act* (MHL 9.46), the law mandates that *"mental health professionals [are] to report to their local director of community services ('DCS') or his/her designees when, in their reasonable professional judgment, one of their patients is 'likely to engage in conduct that would result in serious harm to self or others'."*[128] The attorney for the gun owner has filed a request for a local hearing and expects his client's 2nd Amendment rights to be fully restored. Interestingly enough, the same attorney said he is hearing other cases like this.

Since this will most likely be ruled an illegal confiscation (if the 2nd Amendment is obeyed), it's too bad that the gun owner has to pay for an attorney to prove it. The state should have to pay for creating asinine and illegal laws.

Beyond this, Secretary of State John Kerry, as representative for the United States, signed onto the UN's Small Arms Trade Treaty during the month of September. Many believe this will open the door to the creation of a national gun registry, making it possible for the federal government to begin gun confiscation as New York and California states have begun doing.

---

[127] http://www.theblaze.com/stories/2013/04/09/a-form-of-gun-confiscation-has-reportedly-begun-in-new-york-state-heres-the-justification-being-used/ (04/10/2013)
[128] Ibid

While the UN's Small Arms Trade Treaty is not something (at this point) that would now affect private ownership of guns, it could become that because of the way amendments are created at a future date.

Beyond this, even if the Senate does not ratify this treaty, I can see the Obama administration going ahead as if they did. Moreover, if the Senate does ratify it, it would immediately mean the creation of a brand new federal agency given the chore of implementing and overseeing aspects of this treaty. The cost to taxpayers would be millions of dollars.

Above all things though, the way the Constitution reads, the United States can only enter into treaties with other sovereign nations. Since when is the UN a sovereign nation? That means that any treaty made with the UN is not binding and illegal. Notice though how progressives pay no attention to these stipulations. They simply keep right on rolling over our rights that are guaranteed under the Constitution.

So, Mr. Obama, what was it you were saying about a system that constrains the government from simply taking weapons out of the hands of law-abiding citizens?

Chapter 19

It's a Politically Correct World

Unfortunately, we are living in a leftist-created politically correct world. Those of us who understand what has been happening and what has pervaded society are speaking out against it. We do so to warn other people before it becomes impossible to see truth. That may not happen at all, in spite of our best efforts.

This book – the second on the topic of political correctness – was written to help folks see the realities of just how bad political correctness is in society. It creates a very poor substitute for God's absolutes with a truth that is based solely on how a person feels about an issue. That is the starting point. From there, people then determine what their reaction to a specific societal issue should be based on how they feel about it.

We've covered a good deal of ground between this book and my previous book on political correctness (*Falling Away*). It would be easy to write more books on the subject using more examples from society, and that may happen. In the meantime, I'm hopeful that the examples provided in this book have not only opened your eyes to the reality of corruption embedded within a politically correct culture, but that you will also now know what to look for so that you can avoid becoming swept up by political correctness. I'm also hoping that you will stand against it based on what you have learned.

The insidiousness of political correctness is absolutely awful. It really helps no one at all, yet there are many who actually believe that it does. They think it levels the playing field, but the problem is that they are always looking *backwards* and thinking in terms of what it will take to make things "equal." That is an impossible thing to measure. No one would ever agree on when that equality would be gained because everyone has a different perspective on it.

Some within the black community would likely argue that it will never equal itself out because there has been too much done to blacks. The people who think like this are harboring hatred when they should be letting it go.

We cannot control what other people think or do. We cannot control what people say and what they believe. We can only control ourselves.

In this way, I am hopeful that this book has opened your eyes enough for you to know that you do not need to play the game of political correctness. If you are white, you do not need to hold your head in shame for what other white people may have done to blacks during the terrible time of slavery here in the U.S.

The Civil War was fought, in part, over the issue of slavery. It was fought here in America. It pitted the north against the south and one can truthfully say that not all whites were in favor of segregation and slavery. Many fought to overturn it and did.

If you're white, you can focus on these facts that played out right here on American soil. As a white person, you owe nothing to anyone and I would ask that you not fall into the trap of believing that the white race somehow must pay for the terrible deeds of those specific whites who came before us.

In my case, my relatives came to this country through Ellis Island long after the Civil War was fought. My grandparents on both sides came here from their own homelands. They arrived, legally entered this country and made America their home. This happened in the early 1920s and I have the proof. They never owned slaves of any ethnicity. They came here with the clothes on their backs and what little money they had and started a life here where they raised their own families. Prior to this, my ancestors were all in various parts of Europe.

If you are black (or another person of color), you have the deliberate choice to continue the hatred or to let it go. It's totally up to you what you do about it. I would hope you would not only do what is best for you, but what is best for society as a whole.

Political correctness pits one race against another. It foists unwritten laws onto society that artificially imbue certain groups with more power than other groups, all due to perceived (and even *real*) sleights that few living today had anything to do with when they first occurred. It is simply an extremely unfair way to try to balance the scales, especially when the end result is not justice, but the immeasurable vainglory of "equality" and "freedom."

We will see where society continues to move. Will more people wake to the fact that Cultural Marxism, in the form of political correctness, has taken over much of society with nothing good to offer? Will people come to realize that the people who have created and are using political correctness are nothing more than snake oil salesmen who ultimately want to destroy the biblical values that this country was founded upon?

We can only hope. However, all of society will likely *not* wake up to these facts. Many will continue along in their blinded stupor, believing that the effects of political correctness are not harmful, but actually beneficial to the "victims" in society. Remember, though, victims are determined under the unwritten code of political correctness and, more often than not, completely self-serving.

People *do* need to wake up to the fact that they have been railroaded by political correctness in society. It is certainly not too late for individuals to come to their senses, but it is doubtful that our entire society will see the light.

In 2 Thessalonians 2:11-12, Paul tells us, "*For this reason God will send upon them a deluding influence so that they will believe what is false, in order that they all may be judged who did not believe the truth, but took pleasure in wickedness.*"

Since Paul starts verse eleven out with the word "for," we need to ask what it's there for; why did Paul say "for"? The answer comes in verse 10 and states, "*because they did not receive the love of the truth so as to be saved.*"

In other words, *because* people (and society as a whole) do not *love* the truth (God's truth) that would lead them to salvation, God sends a delusion that causes them to believe "what is false." Is it God's fault?

No, He understands that people do not *want* the truth at all. They continually reject it so, based on that, He simply sends them a delusion that makes it easier for them to believe the lie that has permeated society.

I believe at least part of that lie is found in political correctness. I hope you also see that and that it must be rejected at all costs because it has no connection to the truth.

There is nothing good within political correctness. It simply pits race against race and gender against gender. Because it pursues "equality" with no real world measurement, it simply winds up creating one injustice after another.

For those who get swallowed up in the lies of the politically correct circus, it is going to be next to impossible to move away from it and reject it in favor of actual truth. Christians must come away from it and then they will be able to lead others out of it into the glorious light of the gospel of grace.

This is our calling and lives hang in the balance.

Chapter 20

Non-Politically Correct Solution

I would be completely remiss if I ended this book without offering at least some kind of solution to the problems we face in this world. If you're *not* a Christian, then the solution I'm pointing out is outlined in the next chapter, which is also the final chapter of this book.

It has come to be the way I end all of my books. There is no more important decision each person can or will make than whether or not to receive the only true salvation that is available, the very salvation that Jesus Christ made possible for us. If you do not know Jesus, then please, I cannot urge you strongly enough, receive His salvation and enter into a life-changing relationship with Him. It means the difference between heaven and hell.

However, if you *are* an authentic Christian, then this chapter will hopefully end on a high note for you. What do we do as authentic Christians who are bound to face increasing erosion of our rights under the U.S. Constitution and greater tyranny from our own government?

There really is only one answer of which I am aware. It is twofold in nature, but it is the answer that the Bible repeatedly gives us as the means to peace in our daily walk with God.

- *Submit to His will in all things*
- *Praise Him in the midst of all things*

Honestly, is there anything else a Christian *can* or *should* do? If we believe that God controls all outcomes and that everything that comes our way will eventually work out according to His will for our good and His glory, how can we *not* submit ourselves to Him and praise Him for all things?

Difficulties of Life

I will admit that this is very difficult for me. In essence, it is the very substance of what being a Christian means. I like being in control as much as possible. When I consider what is ahead of us, I *do* become somewhat nervous and apprehensive. Will the government be able to successfully remove our guns from society? If so, what will that mean for me and my ability to protect my family from home invasions, for instance?

Is the Lord protecting me anyway? If so, should I not be casting all my cares on Him because He cares for me? That's what Peter tells us in 1 Peter 5:7. But then Paul tells us that the man who does not care for his own household is worse than an infidel (cf. 1 Timothy 5:8). That means quite a bit in reality, from things like providing food and a roof overhead to issues that revolve around safety. What do I do? How about if work becomes so difficult that we lose our jobs?

All of these things and more are the things that concern me. Some would say I'm borrowing trouble that may never come. Others would say that I should not be concerned about those things *until* they come.

The truth is that we live in a world that is constantly changing and becoming even more evil. We have talked about these things throughout these pages. Yet, in spite of everything, God is fully in control of all outcomes. If we are His – as the Bible assures us we are through faith in the finished work of Christ – then will He not provide? Will He not take care of us?

Can We Trust God or Not?

The only and obvious answer is that He *will*. In the here and now, I can and should *prepare* for coming hardships. I should do what I can to have things in my pantry and storehouse that will keep us going for up to three months – more if I can swing it. It is important that each person do what they can in order to *not* have to depend upon the government or others when the bottom falls out.

At the same time, we make these preparations knowing that God watches over us and cares for us. We do not know what will happen tomorrow. We do not know how far into the future total financial collapse may be. We do not know when the Rapture will occur, nor do we know when the Tribulation will begin.

Until these things occur, we also do not know how bad things will become for the average person, do we? There really is no way to know.

I believe there are many portions of Scripture that speak to the need to trust Him and let Him deal with the problems that He allows to come into our lives. Let me close this chapter by focusing on wisdom from one of the Psalms. Memorize this. Take it with you in your heart wherever you go. Learn to let it speak to you as you contemplate the problems that face your life.

The only solution to any problem we face is *God*. The only solution to any nervousness, fear, or trepidation we experience is *God*. The only solution for whatever comes into our life that brings with it sorrow, tragedy, or abysmal problems are with God. He and He alone is the answer.

It is up to us to submit these problems and difficulties to Him until we can freely and completely release them into His care. That is a must, and it truly separates those who merely say they are Christians from those who actually are Christians.

Psalm 100

Shout joyfully to the Lord, all the earth.

Serve the Lord with gladness;

Come before Him with joyful singing.

Know that the Lord Himself is God;

It is He who has made us, and not we ourselves;

We are His people and the sheep of His pasture.

Enter His gates with thanksgiving

And His courts with praise.

Give thanks to Him, bless His name.

For the Lord is good;

His lovingkindness is everlasting

And His faithfulness to all generations.

This is what we are to do. We are to first of all *shout,* and we are to shout with joy *to* the Lord. The Psalmist is literally commanding everything on the earth to call out to God with *praise*. That should be our first and continuous order of business.

Paul emphasizes this as well when he says that we should praise God in *all* things (cf. 1 Thessalonians 5:18). In doing so, we are recognizing that God is *in charge* of our lives.

But some might say, *"That is very difficult to believe!"* Yes, I know it is, but because we have a challenging time believing in something does not mean that we give up trying to believe it. It means that we have to persevere that much more until that fear turns to belief and belief turns to knowledge.

We should praise God in all things. Difficult, but it must be done if we are to exercise faith in God and His control over our lives.

Next, we should *serve* the Lord, and we should do this how? We should serve Him with *gladness*. That again is often very difficult, but there is only one solution to our doubts: *perseverance*. We cannot give up here. We must continuously praise God with everything that is within us so that we will find ourselves emotionally removed from the circumstances that wish to bind us in fear.

The Psalmist then goes on to say that our lives should be filled with joyful singing and we should come to recognize that God is our *Lord*. He is our Shepherd, and like the loving and careful shepherd who takes care of *all* the sheep in His care, God will surely do the same thing with us.

Since we are the sheep of *His* pasture, it is logical then to assume that He is the One who provides for us. His eye is always on us, our troubles, and our lives in general. He does not forget us and is always mindful of our frailties.

The Psalmist then reminds us that God is *good*. He is far more than good, but this one word helps us understand that *because* of the fact that He is good, He will do what is best for us. He is not some evil being bent on teasing us unmercifully until we bend to His deceitful will!

God has only our best interests in His heart and seeks to bring those to fruition every day. The Psalmist ends with two declarations. God's lovingkindness will never fail because it is eternal, and He is faithful to authentic Christians in *every* generation. These are two truths upon which Christians stand. We must never forget them. We must always be aware of them and we must allow these truths to penetrate our hearts and lives in order that He will be glorified in and through us.

God is not going to leave us, and when we are tempted to think that He has or will, we need to remind ourselves of the truth of Scripture. Romans 8 tells us He will never leave or forsake us and that because we are in Christ, not only are we not on the receiving end of God's condemnation, but we will *never* be on the receiving end of it!

God is good. His goodness lasts forever and it is always directed toward those who are part of His family – those who are in relationship to Jesus Christ.

The only solution that I am aware of related to the problems this life throws at us is found in submitting our will to God and praising Him in all things. Try as I might, I have found no other Scriptural remedy for life's problems, and even though I do not live these things perfectly, God always brings me back to them.

My prayer for you is that He will do the same thing for you so that your life will be filled with His peace, you will learn to trust Him in all things, and you will be freed to fulfill the Great Commission. May He be praised forever.

Chapter 21

Non-Politically Correct Future

D o you know *when* you will die? Are you aware of the *day* and *hour* when you will slip from this life into eternity? I'm betting you are not privy to that information. So why are you living as if you **_do_** *know when it will happen?* Putting a decision about Jesus off until another day is taking a huge chance because of the fact that you do not know when you will die. That is plainly simple, and logic alone demands that you do not put this decision off. Yet you do, because the thought of becoming a Christian makes you feel uncomfortable.

You wrongly believe that to become a Christian means that you have to change in a major way *before* Jesus will accept you. It means to you giving up the things you love now because if you love them, then obviously they are wrong and God does not love them.

You are putting the cart before the horse. You must understand that God is not rejecting you. He is not standing there, tapping His foot, demanding that you eliminate those things that He does not like before you can come to Him for salvation.

If you (or anyone) could do that, you would not *need* His salvation at all. It is because you and I do things that are not pleasing to Him that we need His salvation.

What do you do that you would like to no longer do? Do you drink excessively until you cannot control it? Do you play around with drugs? Do you eat too much food until you have become overweight, lethargic and sickly?

What other things are in your life that you do not like? Are you drawn to illicit extra-marital affairs? Do you have a problem with lust? Are you a shopaholic? Do you tend to tell lies a great deal because it makes you feel important, or to hide things about your life?

Do you find that you do not like people and you would prefer to be around animals or out in the woods than around people? Are you a workaholic? Do you place a high value on money and you find that you work very hard to obtain it?

Here's the problem. The enemy of our souls comes to us and tells us that God will never accept us until we get rid of those things. He lies to us that God essentially wants us "perfect" before He will be willing to meet us and grant us eternal life. This is completely untrue.

The other lie that our enemy tells us is that we should not become a Christian because the fun in our life will fly out the door. We will no longer be able to drink or do the fun things we enjoy now. We start to think that coming to God means becoming a doormat for people and having to fill our life with things we do not want to *ever* do.

These are all lies, and unfortunately, too many people believe them. First of all, God does not expect you to be "perfect" before you come to Him for salvation. If that were the case, no one would be able to ever approach Him.

Secondly, God does not say that He is going to take away all the things we enjoy and replace them with things we hate. What is wrong with enjoying the lake on your boat? What is wrong with spending a day with the family fishing or just relaxing in the mountains? There is nothing wrong with these things.

What God *will* do is begin to remove the things that have ensnared you so that life is actually draining from you, but you are not aware of it. For instance, maybe you drink excessively and you have tried everything you can think of to quit. You have gone to AA meetings, spent thousands of dollars on this program or that, and you have even used your own will power to free yourself from the addiction to alcohol, all to no avail.

The question is not: *do I need to quit before I come to Jesus?* The question is: *am I willing to allow Him to work in and through me to take away the addiction I have to alcohol?* Do you see the difference? Are you willing to allow Him to work in you to break that addiction so that you will become a healthier person, one who is able to think straight and one who learns to rely on Him for strength? That is all He wants you to be able to do. He knows you cannot break that addiction (or any addiction for that matter) with your own strength and willpower. Are you willing to allow Him to do it in and through you?

What if you are a workaholic? What if you have "things" like a boat, a house in Cancun, a large bank account, four cars, and more? Do you think that God is going to ask you to give it up, or worse, do you think that God will simply come in and take all of that from you? I know of nothing in Scripture that tells us He will do that.

What God will do with all of those who come to Him trusting Him for salvation is one thing, which begins the moment we receive salvation and will continue until the day we stand before Him. He will begin to create within us the character of Jesus (cf. Ephesians 2:10).

Here is a verse from the Old Testament that was said originally through the prophet Ezekiel to the people of Israel. While this was specifically stated to the Jews, it is applicable to all who receive salvation through Jesus Christ.

"I will give you a new heart and put a new spirit within you; I will take the heart of stone out of your flesh and give you a heart of flesh. I will put My Spirit within you and cause you to walk in My statutes, and you will keep My judgments and do them" (Ezekiel 36:26-27).

God is speaking here through Ezekiel, and He is saying that He will give the people a new heart of flesh, removing that old heart of stone. This is God's responsibility. God is the One who makes that happen. We are told in the book of Hebrews that God is the Author and Finisher of our faith (cf. Hebrews 12:2). This tells me that God is the One who changes me from within so that over time, my desires are slowly turned into His desires.

I recall years ago thinking that God wanted to do everything in my life that I did not want Him to do. I fell into the asinine belief that He wanted to change everything about me. What I learned is that yes, there are things that God does want to change about me. However, there is a lot that God originally gave me that He has also enhanced and used for His glory.

Maybe you are a workaholic who thinks that working hard is something God does not want you to do. This is not necessarily the case.

He may have given you the ability and the knowledge to work in the area of finance for a great purpose. All He may wind up doing is dialing back your workaholic tendencies so that you have more time to enjoy your family and study His Word.

But you say you smoke, or drink, or use illegal drugs, and you don't want to give those up. As I stated, you can't give those up under your own power, and the fact that you have tried so many times has proven it to you.

But God knows what is and what is not good for you. Are you willing to *allow* Him to work in you to change your desires so that you no longer want to smoke, use illegal drugs, or drink nearly as much?

Then you say that you believe God wants to make you a Christian so you can become miserable. Isn't that what most Christians are – miserable? Not the Christians I know, and certainly not me, my wife, or our children.

Where does the Bible say that God wants us miserable? You will not find it. What God wants is for us to be blessed, and that begins when we receive salvation from His hand.

You know, if we would stop and take the time to consider the fact that this life is exceedingly short if we compare it to eternity, we will then realize that there is nothing so important that it should keep us from receiving Jesus as Savior and Lord.

Unfortunately, too many people do not consider the brevity of life. They think they will live forever, or at the very least, they will die when they are really old and gray. That will come too soon. Even though I have just recently turned 54, it still truly seems like yesterday that I was a young boy fishing in the Delaware River near Hobart, New York. There I spent many Saturdays fishing and simply enjoying being outdoors. How did life go by so very quickly? How could that have happened?

It has happened, and I am at a point in life where not only do I realize that this life is short, but I actually look forward to spending eternity with Jesus after this life. Does that sound morbid to you? It shouldn't, because by comparing this life to eternity, we should get a sense of what is truly important.

God does not expect us to become Mother Theresas. He does not necessarily expect us to give up everything and become missionaries in outer Mongolia. What God expects is for us to simply allow Him to change our character as He sees fit.

Over time, we may well find that we have simply stopped swearing without realizing it. Our desire for cigarettes or alcohol has nearly evaporated. Illicit affairs no longer enter the picture.

We also may find that some of the things we want to eliminate in our life become more pronounced. Often the enemy will do this to cause us to focus on something that God is not even doing in our lives at that point. It causes tension, frustration, and self-anger.

If you have gotten to this point in your life and you have not dealt with the question about Jesus, it is about time you do so. You need to stop what you are doing and realize a couple of things before you go through another minute in this life.

- **Sinner**: you need to realize that you are a sinner. You have sinned and you will continue to sin. Sin is breaking the laws that God has set up. We all sin. We have all broken God's laws and that breaks any connection we might have had with God. Sin pushes us away from Him.

   Romans 3:23 says, *"For all have sinned, and come short of the glory of God."* That means you and that means me. All means all. That is the first step. We need to recognize and agree with God that yes, we are sinners. I'm a sinner. You are a sinner. This results in God's anger, what the Bible terms "wrath."

- **God's Wrath**: Romans 1:18 says, "*For the wrath of God is revealed from heaven against all ungodliness and unrighteousness of men, who suppress the truth in unrighteousness.*"

This is as much a fact as the truth that we are all sinners. Because we are sinners – by breaking God's law(s) – God has every right to be angry with us and ultimately destroy that which is sinful. If we choose to remain "in" our sinful states throughout this life, we will – unfortunately – be destroyed with the rest of sin.

Fortunately, there *is* a remedy, and it is salvation.

- **God's Gift**: In the sixteenth chapter of Acts, a jailer asks Paul this famous question: *what must I do to be saved?* The question was asked because Paul and Barnabas had been imprisoned, and while there, they began singing praises to God.

God then sent a powerful earthquake that opened the doors to all the prison cells, yet no one escaped. When the jailer arrived, he saw that everyone was still in their cells, and after seeing that miracle (what prisoner would not want to escape from prison?), turned and asked what he must do to be saved. He was speaking of the spiritual aspect of things. He wanted to know how he could be guaranteed eternal life.

The answer Paul gave the man was, "*Believe on the Lord Jesus Christ, and thou shalt be saved, and thy house*" (Acts 16:31).

This is not head knowledge or intellectual assent. This is *believing from the heart.* In fact, Paul makes a very similar statement in another book he wrote, Romans. He says, "*That if thou shalt confess with thy mouth the Lord Jesus, and shalt believe in thine heart that God hath raised him from the dead, thou shalt be saved. For with the heart man believeth unto righteousness; and with the mouth confession is made unto salvation*" (Romans 10:9-10).

When we fully believe something, we confess that it is true. It must begin in the heart because that is where the will is located. We must want to believe. We must endeavor to believe. We must seek to believe.

We must stop giving ourselves all the reasons to deny or ignore Jesus. As God, He became a Man, born of a virgin. He clothed Himself with humanity that He might show us how to live, and in so doing, would keep every portion of the law.

If Jesus was capable of keeping every portion of the law, then He would be found worthy to become a sacrifice for our sin – yours and mine. If He became a sacrifice for our sin, then all that we must do is embrace Him and His sacrificial death.

In short then, to become saved we must:

1. Admit (we sin)
2. Repent (want to turn away from it)
3. Believe (that Jesus is the answer)
4. Embrace (the truth about Jesus)

We **admit** that we are sinner, that we have sinned. This is nothing more than agreeing with God that we have broken His law. Can you honestly say that you have not broken God's law? If you admit to breaking even the "smallest" law, then you are a lawbreaker.

After we admit that we have sinned, the next step is found in **repenting**. Some believe that repenting is actually moving away from sin. This author believes that it is a willingness to move away from sin, and there is a difference.

As we have already discussed, it is impossible to stop sinning. Human beings simply cannot do it because as long as we live, we will have a sin nature, which is something within us that gives us a propensity to sin. As long as we have this inner propensity to sin or break God's laws, we will never be perfect in this life.

We cannot one day say, "Lord, I promise to stop sinning." If we do that, we are only kidding ourselves and setting ourselves up for major failure. We cannot stop sinning in this life. The most we can do is *want* to stop sinning and then spend the rest of our lives allowing God to create the character of Jesus within us, slowly, little by little.

Repenting is to decide that you no longer want to do the things that keep us out of heaven. We no longer wish to break God's laws. It is not promising God that we will never sin again.

Once we admit, then repent, we must **believe**. This is one of the most difficult things to do because believing that Jesus died in our place, that He lived a perfectly sinless life, is extremely difficult to believe. Our minds cannot grasp that truth. We must ask God to open our eyes to that truth so that we can embrace it.

While on the cross next to Jesus, the one thief joined the other thief in ridiculing Jesus. Then, all of a sudden – as we read in Luke 23 – this same thief that had just been ridiculing Him now turned to Him with a new understanding.

It was this new understanding that prompted the thief to say to Jesus, *"Lord, remember me when you come into your Kingdom."* Jesus looked at the man and responded to him, *"Today, you will be with me in paradise."*

What had occurred in the mind and heart of that thief from one moment to the next? One thing, and that one thing was that God opened the thief's eyes so that he could see the truth. It was as if the blinders fell off and he now saw and understood who Jesus was, even to the most cursory degree that Jesus was dying not for Himself, but for others.

It was this understanding, this awareness, which prompted the man to ask Jesus to simply be remembered. Jesus went way beyond it to promise the man that he would be with Jesus that day in paradise.

Please notice in Luke 23 that there is nothing in the chapter that tells us that the man promised Jesus he would give up sin, or that he would never sin again. There is nothing that tells us that thief took the time to enter into a final deathbed confession of his sins so that he could be absolved.

The thief made no promises to Jesus at all. What he experienced was the truth of who Jesus was and what Jesus accomplished for humanity. Jesus accomplished what we cannot. What is left is for each person to *admit, repent, believe*, and *embrace*.

Let me clarify here that though we do not see any verbal repentance from the thief, we know that he did repent. He admitted as well. How can we know this? It is simply due to the thief's complete about-face with respect to his attitude toward Jesus. One minute, he was ridiculing Jesus, and the next, embracing Him. This is important. There is no way he could have or would have *embraced* Jesus had he not been humbled by the truth *about* Jesus.

Once the thief saw the truth, he was instantly humbled. Within himself, he knew that he was a sinner, and in fact the text states that this is what he told the other thief dying next to him. *"But the other answering rebuked him, saying, Dost not thou fear God, seeing thou art in the same condemnation? And we indeed justly; for we receive the due reward of our deeds: but this man hath done nothing amiss*" (Luke 23:40-41). Something happened within the heart of the one thief. In one moment, the thief went from harassing Jesus to recognizing his own sinfulness and then ultimately asking for grace, which was freely given to him.

Whether he said it or not, the thief went from haughtiness to humility in a very short space of time, and it was all because he saw the truth about Jesus. That truth helped him realize that he deserved his death and what would happen to him after death. He understood that Jesus did not deserve death.

From here, the thief fully embraced the truth about Jesus and was rewarded with eternal life because of it. He did not come off the cross to be water baptized. He did not list a long litany of offenses against God. He recognized the truth about Jesus, was humbled, and embraced that truth!

This is what each of us needs to do. We cannot give in to the lie that tells us that we are not good enough, or we have not given up enough before God will accept us. We must reject the lie that says we must somehow earn our salvation.

Jesus has done everything that is necessary to make salvation available to us. The only thing that is left for us is to see the truth. Once we see that truth, it should humble us to the point of embracing Jesus and all that He stands for and is to us.

The eighth chapter of Romans begins with the fact that all who trust Jesus for salvation are no longer condemned...*ever*. All of my sins – past, present, and future – have not only been forgiven, but canceled. It is because of my faith in the atonement (death) of Jesus that God is able to cancel all of my sins, even the ones that I have not committed yet. This does not make me eager to commit them. It makes me want to do what I can to avoid sinning.

If you do not know Jesus, please do not put down this book without deliberately *believing* that He is God, that He died for you by the shedding of His blood on the cross, and that He rose three days later because death could not keep Him. Do you believe that? If you do not yet believe it, do you *want* to believe it? If so, then simply ask God to help you come to believe all that Jesus is and all that He has accomplished for you. God will answer your prayers and you may either receive instantaneous awareness of all that Jesus is and has done, or it may be a *growing* awareness over time. In either case, it is the most important decision you will ever make.

Turn to Him now and pray for knowledge of the truth and an ability to embrace it. Please. He is waiting for you.

Ask Yourself:

1. Do you *know* Jesus? Are you in *relationship* with Him? Have you had a spiritual transaction according to John 3?
2. Do you *want* to receive eternal life through the only salvation that is available?
3. Do you believe that Jesus is God the Son, who was born of a virgin, lived a sinless life, died a bloody and gruesome death to pay for your sin, was buried, and rose again on the third day? Do you *believe* this?
4. Do you *want* to *embrace* the truth from #3?
5. Pray that God will open your eyes and provide you with the faith to begin believing the truth about Jesus. Ask Him to help your faith embrace the truth, realizing that you are not good enough to save yourself and that your sin will keep you out of God's Kingdom without His salvation.
6. Pray as if your life depended upon it because *it does*!
7. If you have prayed to receive Jesus as Savior and Lord, please write to me. I want to send you some materials at *no charge or obligation*. Write to me at **fred_deruvo@hotmail.com** and sign up for our free bimonthly newsletter at **www.studygrowknow.com**

Stop by our Internet page...http://studygrowknow.com

And check out our books...**FREE** to download.

www.ingramcontent.com/pod-product-compliance
Lightning Source LLC
Chambersburg PA
CBHW080049280326

41934CB00014B/3260